Leaning on
GATES

Seamus O'Rourke is an award-winning writer, director and actor from Co. Leitrim. He tours Ireland regularly with his own self-penned shows. Seamus has had millions of hits across his social media pages for his recitations and sketches. He is a regular contributor on RTÉ Radio 1. *Leaning on Gates* takes up where his first popular memoir, *Standing in Gaps*, ends.

Leaning on
GATES

SEAMUS O'ROURKE

Gill Books

Gill Books
Hume Avenue
Park West
Dublin 12
www.gillbooks.ie

Gill Books is an imprint of M.H. Gill and Co.

9781804580370

Edited by Bernadette Kearns
Proofread by Esther Ní Dhonnacha
Printed and bound in the UK using 100%
renewable electricity at CPI Group (UK) Ltd
This book is typeset in Sabon.

*The paper used in this book comes from the
wood pulp of sustainably managed forests.*

A CIP catalogue record for this book is
available from the British Library.

5 4 3 2 1

MIX
Paper | Supporting
responsible forestry
FSC
www.fsc.org   FSC® C171272

Dedicated to my mother and father

Contents

Foreword

I had no intention of writing another book. My first memoir, *Standing in Gaps*, was about a time almost forgotten – about a me I hardly remember and an innocence that couldn't be continued. It offended no one. A second instalment would have to deal with the older me – a me I *can* remember – a me that sends a rush of blood to my jowls every time I think about him. It's one thing being a young naïve boy in '70s Leitrim, but to recount the downright stupidity of my older self in the shoulder-padded '80s is a different thing altogether. I could lie and paint a handsome picture of a lad who had just turned eighteen, follow him till he was on the threshold of twenty-five; put a nostalgic spin on that Ireland – on that me. But that wouldn't work. I'd be found out. My readers are too astute – I think they'd spot a major fabrication.

And, of course, there's another very good reason not to write about that part of my life. Not very much happened in that part of my life. At least, not much happened to *me*. So, why do I persist in writing another memoir? Well, it's for you. Because you were there too. I might not mention your name, but you'll see yourself in there. You had to be there. Surely, I wasn't the only one fumbling? The only one being rejected? Surely, I wasn't the only one falling in and out of love – in my head. We were all there, and from what I can recall, we were all just doing our best. Of course, it was embarrassing and stupid, and, let's face it, at times, not much fun. But if we did everything right as youngsters, we'd have nothing to write about. Certainly, I'd have nothing to write about. Who wants to read about success – someone succeeding? Someone being careful and always doing the right thing and driving their mother to Mass? No! We want to read about driving our mothers mad. And our fathers. And mostly ... ourselves.

My father is all over these pages. Every time I sat down to write, there he was – looking out at me, wondering had I nothing better to do. Maybe I'm writing to bring him back – to lock horns with him once more. Because, although he's gone 21 years, I still miss him. I still think about him every day, and I'm sure he'd love to get a dig in about me putting him in a book. He wouldn't want to be in a book – any book. 'I'd rather be in Drumshangore Bog!' he'd say. But he has no choice – he's in it now. And a good job, because he's the one who mostly filled those pages of my life – without him, there'd be no book.

And there'd be no book without my mother. She'll kill me. 'Molafuster me,' as she'd say herself – because, in the book, she's mostly giving out. Not that she was always giving out, but because she could give out in the most poetic way – a way that always stuck. And if my father was the bridge of our ship back then, my mother was the sails. She's the one who caught the wind and moved us forward and sideways and every way – any way but still! They were an unlikely couple – an extraordinary combination. Our ship. Our sails. And sometimes our seas.

And then you have the bloody '80s! What a gobshite of a decade that was. The decade when Ireland invited America over on holidays and it never quit raining – with the good white runners destroyed. It was cultural chaos – a musical traffic jam. Like we were being lapped by America in a donkey derby ... and there's nothing worse than looking up a Yank's ass as it strides for home! God help us, we hadn't got a chance!

Then factor in Leitrim and no love or contraception – only ones coming out from Confession. What kind of a book could ya pull from that? A funny one, I hope. One that might not make the Booker Prize, but might remind you of you. At my expense, of course ... and Mammy's and all the other characters who were interesting enough to get caught between these covers.

So, here it is. As honest and as lively as I can get it. It has been painful going back. Not in a sad or tragic way, but I had to open up old sores to find it. Sores, full of the pus of my youth. And it's all true! I couldn't make it up – I'm not that good.

Wake up

There I was ... being violently awoken by my mother.

'Are ya awake? It's nearly half eight!'

I wasn't fully awake ... I was a young fella and could sleep for Ireland at the time. My mother was my alarm clock. She could do gentle: 'Are ya up?' She could be slightly more hurried: 'I say, are you up?' And then she could be wholly unpleasant: 'I'm not going to call you again! Will ya get up for work or you'll be late! Lying in bed like Methuselah ... or one of the McCafferys!'

Poor auld Methuselah used to get shoved into sentences in our house for dramatic purposes only. No one knew who, what or where he came out of – but his name had a nice ring to it and words of leverage were needed to get a young lad out of bed in the mornings. It was a Friday morning. Yesterday, I was seventeen – today I was not. But there was no time for birthday joviality and me late for work. I got up, put on my clothes, went downstairs, ate a feed of porridge, grabbed an armful of sandwiches that my mother had made and went out the door. I was not late for work – I was never late for work. No one in our house was ever late for work.

Our house (the house we were living in) was soon to be called the 'old house' because we had built a new house in front of it – a modern bungalow to replace the humble storey-and-a-half farmhouse that had stood for hundreds of years without ever being replaced before. The main reason for the new house was that there was no bathroom in the old one. We would be the first O'Rourkes to do our business inside. That was something to look forward to. And we had built the new house ourselves – a project spanning over two years. A kiss-me-arse sort of job that only my father would take on. My father was Jim Rourke – or Jim O'Rourke, depending on where you were coming from – and he was a man of great vision. He couldn't see what would be wrong with us building our own house. There was no such word as *stress* back then, but 'this bloody house with this bloody L' had taken its toll on all of us. The 'L' meaning it was an L-shaped house and not just a straight bungalow. The Auld Lad was in line for an honorary degree in head scratching and giving out, and my mother had started working in the local textile factory in Newtowngore to help pay off the £12,000 county council loan. I was an apprentice carpenter but had only ever made fitted kitchens, and my brother, Kevin, was the farmer. Well, we were all farmers of sorts. When it came to hay time or the bog or moving cattle – we were all brought in to help, even my sisters. Margaret, who was in Dublin, and the youngest, Geraldine, who was still at school, were summoned, when available, to stand in gaps and make tea for the men and join in the ker-fuffle that always went on around our place. We farmed bad land well – a Leitrim man's downfall – and only a few acres in the whole lot. Growing up in Leitrim in the '80s was like trying to hold your ground in quicksand. It was unstable. *We* were all unstable, but we thought we were the cow's tit.

I went to work – driving my recently acquired love-mobile to Carrigallen – and opened the factory for Tommy Reilly. Tommy Reilly made these newfangled fitted kitchens in this newfangled factory, that had been built a few years before. I had been with him for almost three years now, and I was so trustworthy, he had given me the keys to open up every morning. I was never late. I didn't drink or smoke or curse or keep lads waiting at the door. I was a rock of sense for my age … and today I turned eighteen and it hadn't taken a whit out of me. Mad for work and challenging myself at every opportunity. I had money in the post office, a full driver's licence, two Under-14 medals for football, three years under my belt as a county Minor and still one to go. I was six foot two and sure that my life was just about to soar. Turning eighteen should have been a time for taking stock, but I didn't. I wasn't one for taking stock.

There had been nothing about my birthday in the house that morning – no time, I suppose – but I was sure there'd be some sort of fuss made of me when I got home. Not that turning eighteen was a big deal in 1983; or that my family, of all families, were into in-house celebrations. But surely they should appreciate the magnitude of my achievements thus far and feel the need to lavish me with roundabout praise? There was never straightforward praise in our house. The best you could hope for was some sort of indirect cryptic remark that might mean something positive, and then again … might not. Maybe it was better if they said nothing? A positive remark might disturb my sullen existence … might destabilise my foreboding, and then I'd have no excuse to sulk or enjoy the trappings of misery which gave me such pleasure at the time. Let's face it, being seventeen or eighteen is no walk in the park – more like a trudge through the cow tracks of a wet field. Whether it was the hormones or the ham sandwiches, I was as dull and as glum a young fella as you could find … with the potential to become downright subdued.

Happy pieces of jigsaw are no use unless you can fit them together. At seventeen/eighteen I was in no mood to start searching for which bit fitted into which. I'd have more like taken out a gun and shot the jigsaw – if I had a gun. Lucky I didn't. I went home after work and Mammy said, 'Happy birthday,' and I said, 'Thanks.' And there was more. Mammy gave me a card with a tenner, and I got a card from my Aunt Peggy with another tenner and a present from Margaret and one from Geraldine. And that was it. I didn't even have the manners to smile or show any emotion or appreciation … only played Sultry Sue all the way. I tried to eat my dinner before the Auld Lad came in as I thought his enthusiasm for my birthday might tip the scales. But he caught me as I was downing the last shovelful of spuds.

'What height is them presses that you're putting in in that kitchen beyond? I think that bloody windowsill is too low.'

And then we were into 34 inches plus the thickness of the top and allow for the tiles … And thank God for measurements and tiles and low windowsills and not having to have a proper conversation with your dad.

.

My father was not quite a farmer nor a fool but came close to proving me wrong on both counts at different times in his life. He's gone over 20 years now, and there's not a day goes by that I don't talk to him or quote him or feed from his legacy. A true man and father of his time ... properly embarrassing to no one but his own. Awkward and straight at the same time. A man with a sense of what was just and what was just nonsense. He had independent thought – a rarity at the time – and he taught us integrity and how to put on an edge. He hated to see someone cutting grass or a hedge or bread with a bad edge. 'Sharpen the knife or the blade and it will do the work.' I never hugged him – or him me – but I do remember sitting on his knee as a child and rubbing his stubbled chin. He rarely went unshaved, but this day he had growth on his face, and I was fascinated by its roughness to the touch. Yet it felt like I was taming him with every stroke. As close and as intimate as a father and son could be. I didn't feel pride or love or joy ... it was just being on my daddy's knee and stopping him from having his tea. I only ever touched his face once after that.

I shook his hand once when I came back from the States in 1986, and he and me mother came down to Shannon airport to meet me. It was a cold day in March, and he had purple hands because of his bad circulation. Mammy hugged me and welcomed me home, and he held out his big purple hand and shook mine and said, 'Was there many on the plane?' The other time I touched his face was when he died. That strange thing people do when they see a corpse ... they touch the hands or make a sign of the cross on someone's forehead. It's an awful act really, taking advantage of someone by touching them when they're dead and they can't respond. But I touched my father's face after he died. It was cold and devoid of life – so I chose to remember when I was just a child, when he bounced me on his knee and said:

Up, up little horsey
Up, up again
How many miles to Dublin?
Four score and ten

And then I touched his stubbled chin and cheeks – when he was mad alive and so was I. When the world was full of wonder for the both of us, before he began to worry about me and my fate and where I should aim and when I should throw. Did he not know to leave me be? But how could he? He loved me too much; he loved us all so much that he had to always throw in his sixpence worth. He was a great father – no hugging or cuggerin' like now; telling childer that they're great and them not even able to put on an edge. The last thing you want is happy contented young people. Sure nothing would ever get done or changed or disturbed if we let them think that they're great and intelligent and well adjusted. Me and my father would continue with and without each other for evermore.

The bottom rung

At last, I was a grown-up. I had survived the child labour, the poverty and the embarrassment of being a farmer's son in Leitrim. It had been claustrophobic, but at least now, I was a young adult – bulging with adulthood and big shoes and leftover ideas. I could have been anywhere else that night, but I wasn't. I was in Carrigallen parish hall, standing against the wall, expecting adulthood to beam me up. That was never going to happen. It was the 11th of March 1983 – a Friday night – my eighteenth birthday! Thankfully, no one knew it was my birthday except me, my mother and my sisters. My father and brother were unaware, as birthdays back then were not really a 'thing'. They caused little distraction or annoyance – or joy. And being in the hall that night only added to the severity of my new-found realisation. I was eighteen and smack bang on the bottom rung!

There was sometimes an air of excitement going into Carrigallen Hall. Like when we went there to see the local play. The Carrigallen Community Players, under the stewardship of Father Patsy Young, were magic. For a couple of weeks every spring the hall was a place of laughter and expression and escapism. The rest of the year it was well-kept, tidy ... and uninspiring. An all-year-round exhibition of tongued and grooved wall panelling and echo. A wooden floor, underused for dancing, badminton, indoor soccer and basketball; a balcony at the back for cups of tea and Pioneer meetings. A side room for snooker and billiards, and just off the main hall, the mineral bar and the shop – empty shelves, price lists and sticky underfoot conditions.

Tonight we were there to support a local social. There was always need for a parish social – a fund-raiser. It might be for a missionary priest who was heading back out on the missions after spending some time at home – back to converting the poor unfortunate, non-Christian heathens of the world. Or a dance for a family whose house got burned. Or a woman whose young husband got killed by a bull – or off his motorbike – or got his leg broke in a football match. Or if someone was going to Lourdes to get cured of an incurable disease. The parish would come together and throw money into the biscuit tin and satisfy themselves that they had done the right thing. These community events would always be held in the Hall and not in the Kilbrackan Arms Hotel, so that those who didn't drink didn't feel intimidated by alcohol-infused friendliness and enthusiasm. A parish social in the Hall was as careful and as timid as a mouse party underneath the floorboards of the county home.

Tom Farrell was the tall, stern officer of the Hall: the caretaker. A middle-aged man up to his furrowed brow in fold-up chairs, Dettol and Emerald sweets. His brown pinstriped suit in perfect parallel with the tongued and grooved surroundings. He was always there. His grumpiness, dutifulness and honesty were never in doubt. He manned the door, the floor, the shop ... and he set the mood. He took no pleasure in being the only responsible adult with lock and key. He did not bend; he did not break, and smiled only for the priest. *And* he was on to young people! He knew the tomfoolery they could get up to; he had enough of the empty Tayto packets and the sweet papers; the smuggled-in bottles of *fun* ... and the chewing gum! Young people were nibbling away at the Hall's very foundations and his job was to call order ... which he did. Luckily, tonight there were no young people – just old people with the youth sucked out of them. There would be no tomfoolery here; just order and control. Tonight, nobody was having fun.

Tonight's charity was floating close to the bottom of the worthy causes barrel. It was for a McKenna man who lost his tractor when his hayshed went on fire. The hayshed got burned, the tractor got burned and he was fierce lucky that the turf shed wasn't burned too. But there was no turf in the turf shed. And there was only hay in one bay of the hayshed. And it wasn't good hay; it was real bad auld fusty hay. And the tractor could have been saved, if it had started. But it didn't start. It couldn't start – because there was no battery in it. McKenna was a lazy, through-other type. A man fond of reading and having opinions on issues that had nothing to do with him. It's hard to have sympathy for a man who left hay lying out in cocks for months, while he was going around discussing the Falklands war! A man who went off to an agricultural show, instead of helping to look for Mrs Boyle that time. And although it turned out that Mrs Boyle wasn't actually lost, he wasn't to know that.

So, no wonder the hall was only quarter full. No wonder some people, like me, were questioning whether they should be there or not. People don't like a smart alec – a fella going about reading and reciting and knowing things and not even a battery in his tractor. And worse than all that, Pat McKenna didn't even bother to dress up for his own charity dance: a pair of soft shoes and wide bell-bottomed trousers and a flowery shirt, opened to well below where it should be opened to. No tie, no jacket – only big open pockets to bring home the money!

'I'm afraid this Pat McKenna is a bit of a skulk,' my mother said without moving her lips. She did that when she was talking to family in public – pretend that she wasn't talking. Open the mouth halfway and produce words not fully formed, while gesturing with her eyebrows and nose. It's a difficult task – trying to converse with your mother in public without moving a muscle. Your instinct is to match her non-mouthing technique with a similar style of your own – only making an even bigger effort to hide it. That's where the cheek scratching comes in; and the turning away in broad body swerves to direct her line of vision to the Kellys – who are looking over – and could follow exactly what was being said … because they spoke the same eye language.

I didn't want to be talking to my mother, or my father, who was also there – him and Tosh Rourke in deep discussion about 'rush lickers'. I was surprised to see them there. My parents didn't usually go to anything that I'd be at. But, of course, it was *me* that was in the wrong place. It was Pat McKenna's social … and I didn't even know who Pat McKenna was. I was there because my sister Margaret had given me a black leather tie for my birthday that day. A skinny tie, like one you'd see on *Top of the Pops* at the time, and I wanted to try it out ... but there was nowhere to go. This was the only gathering I could find. It was 1983 – a Friday night – in South Leitrim. A world of auld ones and misfits and Pat Fitz ... all painfully waiting for the band.

The band were called the Bandoleros – a quartet of farmers, mechanics and factory workers. One of them was running late – the drummer. He didn't look late; he just looked like someone who didn't want to be there. He got into position behind his drums – adjusted and tightened for effect – looked to the other three and went 'Two, three, four ...' and that was it. That was the best of it – a band that was at its best before it started. The Bandoleros always played at Carrigallen socials, because the Bandoleros were always available; they threw out waltzes and foxtrots, like an unhappy wait-ress in a fair-day eatin' house slappin' watery mashed spuds onto everyone's plate. This was music with no sign of hope or fun or even a key change – bringing musical mediocrity to new levels of despair. What was I doing there?

I tried to ignore my mother's sudden animation as she saw Pat Fitzpatrick taking to the floor looking for a woman. Pat was heading to the uppity section for a dance partner, and because Pat was our neighbour, my mother seemed to take ownership of his current slightly comic adventure. She knew him too well. She also knew he only wanted a good one: a teacher or a woman married to a teacher, or one married to a department man or some other big job. But she'd have to be a good dancer too!

Pat Fitzpatrick was a bachelor who loved dancing. We called him 'Pat Fitz' or 'Pat Fitch', and he used to go to dances with my father, Michael Lee and Eugene O'Kelly thirty years before. Pat watched them slip into marriage and families and feeding hordes of childer and bringing childer to Mass and football matches and Irish dancing. Pat didn't want that. He had his plate full with the farm and the cows and the mother. Only, the mother had got old and was not going as well as she had in years gone by. He had recently got in the phone, and for a while, he couldn't leave the house, because the mother didn't know how to answer it! She used to say, 'Who's that?' when the phone would ring out in the hall ... and her still in the kitchen. It took Pat a long time to get her on to answering the phone by going out to the hall and picking it up. Now he was free. And now he was looking for Mrs Ward – she was a good dancer, a teacher and married to a department man. Pat was a kind of a department man himself. He was mostly a farmer, but he had worked part-time for the Department of Agriculture, washing cattle for the warble fly – a cattle grub prevalent in the early '70s. My father always said, 'The warble fly was the making of Pat.' When he finally got his hands on Mrs Ward, this part-time department man and the department man's wife opened the dancing at Pat McKenna's social and not a warble fly in sight.

The small crowd were slow to follow, partly because of the terrible music, partly because of the debatable cause; but mostly because there was a heavy cloud hanging over Carrigallen Hall, over Leitrim, over the whole Irish countryside – it was called the 1980s.

Joe 'Clamping' Maguire

Only a handful of couples danced the opening few dances at Pat McKenna's social. Only the brave and the desperate ventured out into our gaze – the categories of movement broad and unfulfilled. Phil Maguire and his wife skipped across the floor like they were looking for a lost heifer: long, sweeping steps and sharp turns – no sign of her anywhere – then, heads up and away again. Pat Fitch and Mrs Ward were more 'giddy-up', more 'tiptoe through the tulips and mind the dandelions'. The McGoverns were bordering on the dangerous, with James showing no mercy to Peggy's backwards stride. Where did they learn it? What hospital of dance had discharged such uncoordinated mayhem? The band didn't help either. But mostly the music and the dancing were two separate reels. I had only ever seen these people at Mass or coming out from Confession. Now they looked like they were on the doorstep of a slaughter house and had to frantically buck-dance their way to safety. Hughie Bradley and Molly reluctantly joined the fray, trying to take the bad look off the small numbers on the floor. But also because they liked dancing, and they liked each other ... something that wasn't always apparent in married couples at the time. Most couples I knew were not accustomed to spending time with each other, mostly choosing hard work over intimacy and rosary beads over love.

Eventually, the band and the dancing slowly deflated to a halt. I heard the trailing off of 'Thank you for dancing. Your next dance will be coming right up ...'; the short ripple of leftover drumbeats; and then ... there was nothing. There was now an unexpected silence ... a muted stillness. Like we had all caught a glimpse of ourselves in the mirror and thought *surely this is not us?* It was no longer a social gathering, but a gathering of socially inept lookers-on, all longing for the comfort of the pigsty or a pitchfork or a cow's backside. We were not suited to recreation or unexplained joy. No, that was for the English or the Americans. Rural Ireland only functioned on hard work and misery. Or provoked by alcohol or a fiery priest or schoolmaster. And there I was, the night my new adult world got handed over to me in the parish hall; a world including my mother, my father, my neighbours and a band called the Bandoleros.

A world as naked and as awkward as I'd ever seen it before. I didn't want this world. I had just turned eighteen. I was wearing a skinny black leather tie that was now tightening like a noose; and all around me were broken-down spirits and forgotten dreams!

Cue the saviour. Well, not exactly a saviour, but a survivor ... someone I could take heart from.

The big double doors at the back of the hall swung open and the wind came in. It was supposed to be Joe 'Clamping' Maguire, but Joe didn't enter on his first attempt. He was fairly full that night and the rhythmic spring of the swing doors had catapulted him back out onto the street and thwarted his eager approach. Joe, however, was a man of great resilience. No matter how drunk he was, he was still going to support Pat McKenna's social ... he was still going to pursue his longstanding longing for a woman ... and most of all, Joe Clamping was going to dance!

In time, one of the doors reopened and Joe's head appeared, the spring-loaded teak pushing hard against his neck, and the Major cigarette in his mouth puffing frantically as the message got sent to the rest of his body that he wasn't fully through. Then, with a slight grimace, a smoke-stained hand appeared over his head and his fight to emerge continued.

'How are yez all doing?' Joe muffled, trying to fill the delay as he excavated himself from the front porch. 'Horrid fuckin' night … no let-up to this rain …' Joe was always incoherent; his guttural unshaped words seldom landed a punch. He had almost muscled his way into the hall … but for his trailing leg. 'The curse of fuck on this hoorin' thing …' And then, 'I'm in, I'm in!' At last, Joe Clamping had made it. He was in. A small victory for some … but an outright miracle given the state of him. There was no welcome, no applause; it was as if people had been coming in and out through doors for years. But, for me, that entrance somehow changed me from my pompous state.

Joe Clamping always looked between fifty and eighty, his dark, greased complexion borne out of a love for the mechanical and the mechanically impaired. He had the face of a harrowed field, with friendly eyes shining out through clouds of constant smoke. He was never without a fag, except when dancing or during long bouts of kissing. His suit climbed on board his sturdy frame every evening at three o'clock, and he headed for McGuckian's or Peter's Inn or the Kilbrackan Arms Hotel. He was, of course, a Drumreilly man, but found that he liked the Carrigallens … and they liked him back. The words 'Up Drumreilly' were never far from his lips.

But only to rattle the football crowd, as he wasn't bothered by borders or sporting rivalries.

Although Joe looked like a simple bachelor, he was as complicated as wire wool. Full of generosity and standing drinks out of turn – then he'd fleece ya in a deal when your head was turned. He'd pull out scrap from your haggard and sell it back to you as iron. He'd auction turf that had gone missing and say, 'It won't do ya a bit a harm.' Joe was always plotting; drink or no, he seldom did a foolish thing ... but always played the fool. He loved people and drink, and women and drink – and even drink on its own. But he was seldom alone.

He had good friends everywhere, according to himself. And he was good friends with his father; till his father died ... then he was lost for a time. Went nowhere for a good while. Didn't even go for fags – so they said. I often wondered what woke him from his grief. What brought him back to people and plastic ducks and singing fish? Joe was renowned for having raffles for good causes – although the good cause was usually himself. He'd buy a book of tickets out of Jack O'Neill's ... hold a duck race down the Mill Race, or head to Enniskillen and buy a singing fish in the joke shop and then challenge ones out for a drink in

Carrigallen to buy a ticket ... interrupt their conversations, cough a half ounce of tar into their face, and say, 'Would ya like to buy a ticket for a singing fish?'

Joe dug graves too; a fierce man in a grave, so they said. He dug for those who hadn't anyone to dig for them and cut sticks for those who didn't like cutting sticks. He was never idle, and out from the time his father died, he was never low. Yes, he spluttered a bit, but he always marched on. It's just that Joe 'Clamping' Maguire marched to a different tune.

Joe made a big deal of Pat McKenna when he first came in. 'A horrid decent man,' he announced. 'Awful thing to happen a man in bed ...' To the untrained ear, this might sound as if Pat McKenna was sleeping with his tractor. But he wasn't. He wasn't even in a relationship with his tractor – the tractor had went on fire while Pat was allegedly in bed. But that was enough talking to Pat McKenna. 'Where ta fuck is the band?' Joe correctly called order to the proceedings. The band were mingling with the crowd, sipping tea out of tiny hall cups and hoping that no one would notice that there was no music. But Joe did. 'Get up and start up them accordions,' Joe blurted. And although, thankfully, there were no accordions or accordion players, the band knew it was time to get back to work.

My mother's eyebrows and forehead were now working frantically to portray her shock at Joe Maguire coming in drunk and shouting and cursing and causing a stir. But I also knew by her contorted gaze that it was more than that. She was saying to me, 'There are mad, dangerous people all around. Don't ever become one of them!' I was the furthest thing from Joe Clamping. A big innocent mug of a young lad, sipping Club Orange through a straw, sweating in the discomfort of my comfortable life. Up until now, my only heroes were Santy Claus, a few footballers and Jesus Christ. Maybe Joe was another?

The band started up again and Joe took off.

'Will ya dance, miss?'

'Maybe later, Joe,' was the usual polite response.

'It won't do ya a bit of harm.'

'Ah no, Joe, not tonight. I have Mass in the morning for me mother.'

Veronica Reilly was more forthright. 'Would ya ever fuck off from about me, Joe.'

Clamping was not perturbed; he was never put off by the hostile backfire.

'Mary Lee, come out and dance; your father is a great friend of mine. I cut sticks for him when he was away with his leg.'

Mary was my sister's friend, a lovely girl with just enough gumption to dance and have the craic with the greatest knave to ever inhabit a suit. They danced; Joe three times her age. Mary squirmed as Joe grabbed her and whispered some Morse code gibberish until they both laughed out loud … neither one knowing why. Others smiled. My mother wasn't sure.

Joe's antics unsettled some. He grabbed and twisted and shaped the world to meet his own needs. He didn't have many needs, but he served them well. And he had a steely determination to carry on, regardless of the obstacles or the opinions put in his way. He could make good fodder out of bad hay. That was his aim – as simple and as basic a human as you could find. For Joe knew from his quarter knowledge of machinery and machines that the simpler they are, the less chance of them breaking down.

I got a lesson that night in the parish hall, as I stood feeling sorry for my lot. Life is not about what we perceive to be great or worthy or worthwhile. Life is in the detail. It's about pushing through the doors, about never surrendering … and maybe sometimes causing a stir.

The tallest of the tall

Saturday mornings were always different in our house. No work to go to, but lots of work to do. The clocks time ignored while we used our own. But this was the morning after Pat McKenna's social and my parents were still soft in the cheeks from being out the night before. Not fully re-coiled to their honest hard-working selves; their public personas not yet back in the drawer. Daddy was at the kitchen table and Mammy was making eggs: boiling them and carting them to the table with bread and tea. Tea which Daddy blew on to cool. He couldn't stick hot tea, but he didn't like much milk. That was Daddy. He sat there trying to digest the goings-on of the night before. Why did it feel so lame? They had done their duty and supported a worthy cause. Or maybe an unworthy one – what difference? But not even the priest turned up. Why was that?

My mother seemed more energised by the antics of Joe Clamping, Packy O'Hara and Robbie Lord. They had stood out at the Carrigallen do. Packy O'Hara was the high king of 'acting the goat' – wound up to the last on half ones and bottles of stout. He had stood tall and slim by the mineral bar, his arms folded up under his chin; swivelling like a lighthouse; smiling, waiting for his prey. And then, with the swiftness of a lizard's tongue, he'd reach out and grab a passer-by … nip their arse or their arm or the fat under their arm. Then he'd quickly retreat and let out a 'Whhhheeeee … sexy auld night!' Some were aroused by this primitive excitement. A roaring match followed – a short exchange of yahoos and squeals from those who needed to let off steam. Everyone knew Packy, and most bought into what they considered his harmless antics. 'Sure, what harm is he doing?' Some didn't. Some chose to ignore.

Robbie Lord was more nuisance than lewd and drunk as forty cats. 'That fella is liable to walk out in front of a car.' He seemed harmless enough to me. Yes, mad for drink, but what young fella wasn't? (Apart from me … and my brother … and the Lees.)

'He's a slave to the drink,' everyone said.

'And a great worker.'

'Fierce nice fella … if you could only know what he was saying.'

A walking contradiction is what he was so ... with an unpredictable streak. People didn't like that in anyone. At least with O'Hara, you knew what you were getting; knew he was always going to grab some intimate fist of flab. Always giving out a squawk in the wrong octave for a fully grown man. 'Any auld buzzying lately?' Sexual connotations to the fore.

We accepted that back then. Because we accepted that some people were kind of mad. That we were all some sort of mad, but that ours was a suppressed madness. Having Packy O'Hara, Joe Clamping and Robbie Lord gave us opportunity to join in ... to let rip ... to be momentarily out of control. And sometimes it felt good. My mother enjoyed seeing it; she always chose comedy over tragedy. It was all good fun. All fine, as long as it was other ones at it and not one of her own.

My mother's Maguire side left her with a taste for fun and comical disorder. Not weighed down with any notions or ambition, she could watch a lad slipping on a banana skin all day. Indeed, all my tendencies for silliness come from her ... and for that I am eternally grateful. I could always get around her with a joke or a smart answer. I could never pull the wool over her eyes completely, but I could make her laugh; and if that didn't work, I could tug on her heartstrings with an earnest word and a mournful sigh. She couldn't help but do everything she could for a poor tortured son. Yes, Mammy was handy enough to get round.

But I knew I never fooled my father. He could see right through me. He could see when I wasn't right; when I was putting on a good face. He could see the fear in me ... He noticed the hesitation, the lack of self-belief. But he was most disturbed when he saw fragments of hope. Hope is a gas. If it's not conducted through a solid channel, it evaporates ... and then hope is nothing. My father wasn't into hope. He had seen enough hope evaporate in his time ... he knew the foolishness of it, and had forgotten the importance of it, especially to poor Leitrim souls. My father liked elements that he could control. Hope wasn't one of them.

He was a realist – between a rock and a hard place of common sense. And he turned his talent into a fine art. A spade would always be a spade, even if it looked like a garden hoe. He could predict the outcome of any adventure, especially one based on hope.

'Sure, how could that work?'

'Yes, it'd be lovely to beat Galway, but them kinda things don't happen.'

And he was mostly right. I hated the predictability of his wisdom. So, there was no hope ... was that it?

My father was between six foot three and six foot four; between handsome and a bit awkward. Long legs up to where his waist should be – but he had no waist, no arse. His two legs joined straight into his body, without even a curve. A body that you could roll up – from his feet up to his head. Of course, no one saw that. He was a fine, tall, handsome man. But I could see the flaws. I was forever scrutinising the physical template of me. The man had no waist, no arse. He had no tail swing. And he had no pivot – pivot is a very underestimated feature in a man. He wasn't athletic – that was my biggest problem. I knew his passed-down genes were going to be the downfall of me. Not his fault or mine. Just two unlucky men. I didn't look like him. Well, maybe a bit in the face; but after that, no. I had loads of arse – enough tall swing for the both of us – and I certainly wasn't thin. In fact, I'd say I had most of his failings, plus a good few of my own.

And my father was my conscience which only turned up for the aftermath.

'What took ya in the first place?'

'Why didn't ya do it this way?'

'Did ya not know that was going to happen?'

A barrage of after-the-fact facts – hindsight to the fore, always. I didn't want false praise, but if he would

only, sometimes, shoot me in the knee or the leg, and
not always in the head or the heart. I've heard over the
years, and especially since his death, that he was proud
of me. That's good. I have no evidence to back that up …
but I hope he was.

He had danced with Mammy the night before out
of duty more than anything else. A surreal moment for
me in my skinny black tie. I'm sure no one batted an
eyelid, but I did. What were they thinking? The tallest
of the tall in Carrigallen dancing with a woman always
claiming, but never reaching, five foot two. It was like
he was wheeling a miniature statue of Our Lady around
the floor. Surely, they didn't have to do that in public?
Mammy smiling the one-two-threes, while he went off
with his head up and from his bellybutton up, it looked
like he was dancing on his own. Of course, it was only
good manners to dance, seeing that it was a dance. But
this wasn't my parents. My parents should know better
than to do such an intimate thing in public!

Their dance should have been limited to their every-
day lives: from the jigs and reels of spring and summer
to the slow waltzes of autumn and winter. In the kitchen,
with their things in the yellow cabinet with the pull-down
flap; the Rayburn range and the side tank; the high-up
mirror where Daddy combed his hair and where Mammy

couldn't see. The calendar with the 'cows' times' and the Sacred Heart lamp on the wall. They could dance in the scullery with the American washing machine and the cold press for the milk and the dinted buckets on the floor. They could dance by the green metal press over the sink with Daddy's shaving things, the veterinary supplies and the bags of blue, the penicillin, the teat dip and the caustic sticks for dehorning calves. Or by the buckets of drinking water for the house cornered by the curling wellingtons and the cat's meow.

My parents could dance their dance in the byre and the hayshed … in the ripples of the cow tracks across the fields. They could dance in the bog and in the meadow, saving the hay and digging the spuds – offending no one as they did. That was their way. They were not suited to stepping out in front of everyone at a parish social. But charity and duty had pulled this reluctant pair to the fore. And to me, a mixed-up brat of a boy at the time, they seemed to suffocate and dull in the smoking light.

My parents weren't odd, they were *specific*; they did things their way. Inside out, and back to front.

Mammy didn't go to the shop; she was always too busy. She didn't like dressing up. She'd throw a good coat over a bad outfit to go to Mass; pull a brush through her hair as she was going out the door, and she would always be the same amount of late. Daddy was never late. Even after primping himself for ages, shaving, combing and putting on the shoes that Mammy had polished. But early waited on late and together they made the best of time!

My father loved the town and going to the shop, and because my mother couldn't be bothered, he was full-time at it. Going to Hylands for the few bits or to Carrigallen of a Saturday night; to McGerty's butcher's for the Sunday meat; and then go into McCann's supermarket ... and by the way ... he'd go to Peter's Inn for a couple of bottles of beer and two half ones of Paddy. He'd have a sensible conversation with Peter, and Pat McGee and Thomas Doonan or Cathal Sheridan – they were younger than him and kept him young and out till near closing time – the meat and the groceries waiting in the car to drive him home. But he was never drunk; never stirred or giddy. The town, and what went on there, was always a light that shone, but never dazed his vision – and in that respect, he was a lucky man.

Love and air

The small green metal cabinet above the sink in the scullery had Daddy's aftershave. The Old Spice to add new spice to a lad heading off to a dance on his own. I was going solo. Not for the first time, but after the embarrassment of Pat McKenna's social, I was now more intent on staying well clear of my family – at least where public appearances were concerned. No parents this time. No brother or sisters. Just me and my rather large headful of expectations. I had over-shaved my very soft un-hairy face: lathered it up with Lifebuoy soap and rubbed the razor around it till it started to get red. Then I let go with the Old Spice for beginners. It was like when my sister Margaret persuaded my brother to stick his willy into a bottle of TCP. Kevin's tiddler had inflamed so much, it got stuck in the neck of the bottle – he was only three! I felt almost as compromised after the Auld Lad's aftershave.

There I was – with my big, inflamed face going off to look at young ones in Bawn. The infamous Wonderland

Ballroom. Once a place of rampant romance, now playing second fiddle to the new disco venues, the Wonderland had had its day. This was a time of great social change, and although the film *Saturday Night Fever* came out six years before in 1977 – a movie that fast-tracked disco to non-disco parts of the world – it was only starting to lay its eggs in Leitrim and west Cavan. The Wonderland was still desperately hanging on to the showband era. One of the few venues left for the likes of Gina, Dale Haze and the Champions, The Memories, Rock Stewart and the Plattermen – all bands with a hint of the modern – interspersed with T.R. Dallas, Margo and Big Tom, reminding us all that we still had the tracks of the wellingtons embroidered on our calves.

This was a Sunday night, and there wouldn't be many about the Wonderland. Sunday night was a quiet night: less people, and yes, less women, but also, less chance of a row. That suited this 18-year-old, who was only going for a look anyway. I wouldn't know what to do if there was a row. How could I act brave while not getting involved? I hated fightin' at dances. Probably because I was no good at it. Couldn't fight me way out of a wet gap. I wasn't afraid, but I was slow. And wouldn't get thick till the next day – that was no use if a row broke out. Some lads could fire up in seconds; be casually drinking a mineral at the mineral bar, and the next thing, you'd see the fizz coming out their eyes. I'd think it was the 7UP or the Cavan Cola, but no, it was the fight in them. Mad for the fight, they'd rush off to a hammering match somewhere out on the dance floor. To save a friend or nail an enemy. I couldn't leave the mineral bar without finishing me Club Orange and me Twix.

I wasn't a fighter, but I wasn't a great lover either. Oh, I had high hopes – I had the same buzzing in me trousers as every other young fella. But, as usual, I overthought it. Wanted to be cool … wanted to be romantic … Ended up being a big lump of lard with a red face, hardly able to move with embarrassment and feeling like everyone could see through me. That they could see my pitiful life, with the bread and jam after the dinner, and the pisspots under the bed and that stupid side tank on the side of our Rayburn range. I was a gobshite, if ever there was one.

I was ready for off. I came downstairs of the old house – we still hadn't moved into the new bungalow (afraid the bliss might be too much for us). My father was reading the paper. Mammy was poking something with a needle.

My brother, Kevin, the farmer, was poking something else with a screwdriver – an outside job brought indoors for the warmth and the running commentary from the Auld Lad. 'That won't work without the right tool. You need the right tool to take that off.' My brother ignored all advice, but the advice continued.

My youngest sister, Geraldine, was trying to get homework done for Monday morning.

'I'm off,' I said.

'Where are ya going?'

'Bawn.'

'At this time?'

'Aye.'

'Would it not fit ya better to be going to bed?'

'It would, but I'm going anyway.' And I did.

My mother said, 'I hope you get a woman,' but she didn't mean that. She really hoped I wouldn't get my hopes up about anything or anyone – I was in the right house for that.

The Wonderland Ballroom in Bawn was a big barn of a place. In fact, it would have made a great barn. There were lots of them around the country. Barns, halls, venues given a lick of paint and called some evocative name: the Wonderland Ballroom, the Ballroom of Romance or the Mayflower. Names to get you randy. But they weren't places full of wonder and romance – they were places full of sweatin' and pushin', and pretending you were enjoying yourself when you weren't. The Wonderland that night was almost empty – like a fancy biscuit tin with only a few plain biscuits going soft in the bottom. It wasn't the place for a lone 18-year-old with the cheeks of a baby and the expectations of a stud: an athlete, a county man, a footballer elite ...

Of course, my overriding problem at the time was that I wasn't a footballer. I had, up until recently, thought I was. And that I had a glorious footballing future ahead of me ... But I hadn't. Whatever I had, it was behind me. I had set out to be a somebody in the football world ... and failed. Not a great aura to be marching about an empty dance hall with, but I seemed to fit right in on that Sunday night. I joined the dregs of a forgotten Ireland, sulking under the glitter ball, the monochrome light absorbing our ambition; the monotony of the music hypnotising one and all ... the train gone and the ticket still in our fist. I had to leave before the nail was driven home.

I went out to what seemed like fourteen acres of car park and sat in my red Opel Kadett Coupe – my pride and joy. I searched for some alternative music: Simon and Garfunkel's *The Concert in Central Park*. I put the cassette in the stereo and spun the tyres of the Opel on the loose gravel. I was not going to join the walking dead of a forgotten world ... I was going to find a disco!

I headed for Cavan town – to the Hotel Kilmore – and drove around the back to another fourteen-acre car park. 'Bridge Over Troubled Water' was coming to a crescendo and I was ready to step into the future. I was at the D-I-S-C-O. I was going to a nightclub. Nightclubs were dance halls with the stabilisers removed. The bar was selling alcohol by the bucketful; the women as scantily clad as the time I saw my mother getting ready for bed – when I was four. The noise, the music, the ultraviolet light – I had never seen so much white. I had stepped into the future. This was me!

I removed my jumper. My skinny black leather tie had found its home. I was as giddy as a suck calf in spring. The music changed ... slowed down. I was only in the door – it was like it was meant to be. I summoned a young woman into my arms ... with my eyes. I had new powers of allure. Her eyes were dazzling ... full of drink ... Oh, right ... so it was the drink. Okay ... I didn't have a problem with that. This woman ... this girl ... didn't have a name, because she wasn't able to talk – she must have been from the non-speaking part of Cavan. Fair enough. And she had fallen in love with me already. Wanted to smooch on the dance floor. I had seen ones at that caper and I was up for that. But then she saw a green drink on a table and she made a dash for that. She must have been on a tonic and needed her medicine. And ... she didn't come back.

But I was fine. I didn't mind. There were loads of women, all equally up for falling down and falling in love. I had done it. I had moved ... stepped forward. I felt as if someone had changed the electric fence, and I was now in on the after-grass: sweet and young and refreshing after-grass. I was never going back to the mineral bar. I was hooked on love ... drunken or other-wise. I could feel the air under my wings. Maybe I could fly ... but could I do it without the fuel of alcohol? That was the next step.

I never wanted to drink. I had some righteous notion that it was for the weak. But look how happy these people were ... And how unrestrained they were. What I wouldn't do to un-restrain myself too. But no, I wouldn't drink. Not now – not tonight! That didn't mean I couldn't capitalise on sweet tender maidens who were a little tipsy. The music changed ... time to strut my stuff. 'Let's Dance' by David Bowie. 'Thriller' by Michael Jackson. The Weather Girls' 'It's Raining Men' ... and I was raining down on all of them!

I never learned to jive or waltz or push a statue of Our Lady. I brought nothing to the traditional dance hall scene, and yet expected so much in return. I thought it was enough to be tall and playing for the county, and having a car ... but it wasn't. What I found at the disco and these newfangled nightclubs was different. More me ... more suited to my suavity. I could see, with a bit of practice, how I could navigate these swirly waters without taking a dagger to myself when I got home. I was at home here amidst the see-through, white, ultra-violet trousers and the skinny leather ties. I was a New Age Man – that's why I didn't fit in in Bawn or at the Wonderland. The Wonderland, me hole! But give me the disco ... I was a duck in a pond at the disco. I just had to dress accordingly ... Time to go to shopping to Mullen market for a mooch around the stalls. Leather jackets, padded shoulders and a place for my new-found wings: wings of love ... and air.

Pull up to the bumper

The red Opel Kadett Coupe that I had bought when I was seventeen was my only achievement in life so far. It shouldn't have been; it should have been way down the list, but because I had failed so miserably at everything else, it was the only thing I could offer up as a positive. And it was one sexy car. Some people called it a sports car, and I didn't argue. But it wasn't a sports car. It had a 1.2-litre engine that wouldn't pull the knickers off an elf; but it had a sleeky body and chrome trim, and unlike its Japanese counterparts at the time, it was made to last. 'A proper car.' So Louie Johnston said, and Louie would know. Him and Pat Magee had a garage in Kivvy, Carrigallen – beside where I worked at the time – and he was forever telling me that I had a great car and to look after it and to not be leaving it at the front of the house where the Auld Lad could reverse into it.

My Auld Lad always parked his Escort at the side of our house as near to the back door as he could get.

When I first got my lovely Opel, I parked it at the front of the house where people could see it from the road. No point having a sexy car if no one could see it. After a few weeks, the Auld Lad decided to go somewhere in his car. He folded himself headfirst into the Escort, and without even looking, reversed around the corner into my precious, lovely red sports car. His excuse? It had never been there before! He had been reversing around that corner for over twenty years and never had to look where he was going until now. This underlined for me that the Auld Lad was a thunderin' eejit – a liability. Of course he didn't mean to do it. And yes, under all the 'What was it doing there?' and 'It was never there before,' he was very upset about it. A big clatty ding in the lovely chrome bumper. What an absolute nuisance of an Auld Lad he was – a danger to have about any house.

He said he'd fix it … that made things worse! His version of fix it and mine were two very different things. My version would be to return it to the way it was before he rammed into it. But his was to attain the services of the aforementioned Messrs Johnston and Magee and to enter into a pullin' and beatin' match, ending with a classic farmers' bumper – a bumper that looked like it spent its life dunting on the cows!

All this was to remind me that my life was a sham.

And it was. And I was right about the bumper. The three-some of Daddy, Johnston and Magee made a sow's ear of it. A total mess or 'mess tattis' as my mother would say. The good car was never the same after. And when Shannen's ass jumped in on the bonnet one foggy night a few months later, my lovely red car's sex appeal disappeared forever. There was no physical damage to me or the ass … but the ass-print in the bonnet was deep and the dint in my self-esteem deeper still. My car and my life needed urgent attention.

There was only one place to go – back to Mullen market where the cheap outweighed the useful and the shiny outshone the wise. Where I could browse through the endless stalls of car accessories. Spotlights, fog lights, lights for lights' sake. Maybe a bull bar on the front might add to my manliness? A spoiler on the back to give me more swagger and style? Or the crème de la crème at the time – anti-static rubber strips to avoid electric shocks while travelling at the speed of light? Any or all of these would deflect the eye from the horrible bumps and dings that I had accumulated this far down the road.

I wasn't sure … my father's sensibility starting to seep into my veins as I wandered around the Mullen throng. I began visualising myself behind a furry dice. What would the Auld Lad say? What odds what he says!

Then my conscience started coming at me for thinking the Auld Lad was such a curse ... that he was the cause of my unhappiness. What did he ever do? Out from wear a cap and always be right. He couldn't help it that he was against people eating crisps and this new yogurt and EasiSingles cheese.

His thing was cabbage. He *loved* cabbage, and because he loved cabbage, there was always cabbage for the dinner. Even Mammy was fed up with cabbage. She tried to sicken him with cabbage one time – gave him cabbage for 23 days running, and on the twenty-fourth day, when she thought he had enough, he said, 'Is there no cabbage?' What would ya do with a lad like that? How could ya go home to that lad with a furry dice or anti-static rubber strips? How could I explain unnecessary accessories to my Auld Lad – good old King Solomon himself?

I bought Dr. Hook's *Greatest Hits* – that's all I bought. It wasn't cabbage, but songs you could cry to ... if you were into crying.

It was now April 1983. Football was starting back ... I had almost forgotten I could play, it was so long from our last game the year before. Back then, there was no winter training. I had never been to a gym – our winter gym-work was foddering cattle and cutting sticks. Our first county Minor game of the year was a challenge against St Mel's College in Longford. It was always strange starting off the year. It was like meeting up with an old friend. Only this year – my last year as a Minor – I had my doubts. My friendship with football was on the rocks. The year before with the county had ended badly, and my confidence needed restoration. That morning, I was made captain for the coming year – a great privilege. That helped. I played okay against the famous college team, and as I was walking off the pitch, a polished priest asked me if I'd like to do my Leaving Certificate at St Mel's? He obviously thought I might bring something to their football team, as I wouldn't do much for their academic profile. I had left school three years earlier – with no regrets – but I was chuffed to be asked. I said I had no intention of doing my Leaving Cert in St Mel's or anywhere else, and he said, 'Well, if you ever change your mind.' I wasn't going to change my mind, but an out-of-the-blue offer can still stir your mind. Working long hours for 60 quid a week wasn't all it was cracked up to be. Playing football every day for a college with the proud footballing history of St Mel's was a nice thought.

I could see the St Mel's lads, and indeed some of my own teammates, watch me as I threw the football gear into the back of my car. They were probably saying,

'Look at him with his fancy car. He did the right thing to quit school, even if he can't spell or put two words together. He has the sexiest car in Ireland.' Or maybe they were saying, 'Look at that clatty dinge in the bumper and the track of the ass in the bonnet – what a complete loser.' I don't know what they were saying or thinking or if they were even thinking anything. What difference? I was back into the football.

I didn't tell them at home what the priest had said. That might be cause for concern … or hope. And we wouldn't want that. Instead, I ventured into our long-awaited new house, at the front of the old house, and wandered around. It was nearly finished. I had a few jobs to do – make the last wardrobe for one of the bed-rooms; hang doors on the hot press; put doors on the coat press and finish tiling the bathroom. Would it ever be done? Would we ever be in? Would it be what we hoped it would be – whatever that was? Were we better off where we were? I'm sure washing yourself at regular intervals isn't all it's cracked up to be – or this peeing indoors. We'd miss the breeze coming in under the door of the outside loo. How long was I going to be in this new house? Not long, I hoped!

For the first time, I felt the need to get away. From here. From this embarrassing life … from me. As bad as my parents were, and they could be fairly embarrassing at times, my main problem was me. I was only half cooked: a big, soft lug of a lad, going around with big notions, and me that was shaping up to being useless at everything. I wasn't a great carpenter – I was a middlin' carpenter. I wasn't a great footballer – I was an average footballer. And I was never going to be a great lover unless I pulled up my socks ... or whatever you pulled up to become one of them. Life up until not that long ago was exciting, interesting and ... bearable. Now it was complicated, embarrassing and a bit pointless. Where was all the good stuff? The girls, the admiration, the top of the milk? I wanted the top of the milk.

The milk always caused a row in our house. We didn't buy milk – the pasteurised milk. We had our own milk from the cows. We milked the cows, kept a drop for the house and some for the calves – and even a saucerful for the cat if it was plentiful – and then sent the rest to the creamery. The drop for the house was put in a gallon can and kept in the cold(ish) press in the scullery. The cream would rise to the top. But take care would anyone use the top of the milk for their porridge or their tea! No, that was for the Auld Lad's tea. A nice bit of cream for Daddy's tea – but not enough to cool the tea, because the Auld Lad liked hot tea. And then he'd take into a blowing match, and sipping it, and making a concert out of the first few mouthfuls of tea every morning and after the dinner and every other time there was sups of tae (as he called them). But he got the cream ... the top of the milk ... always. Or the priest got it when he came. Or the visitors. Or Granny. Granny got the most cream. Mammy'd riffle it into Granny's good cup. She'd nearly sicken Granny with the top of the milk ... just to let her know that our house was a house full of 'the top of the milk'. And maybe it was ... but not always.

Jesus, Mary and Joseph

A man by the name of Don Tidey was kidnapped by the IRA in Dublin on the 24th of November 1983. We had never heard of him before. He was an executive for Quinnsworth, which was a forerunner to all these big supermarket chains that we have now. We still hadn't heard of him. He wasn't a famous man, and we didn't pass much remark on news items – they didn't affect us. We were numb to the mention of trouble and the Troubles. Numb to bombs, shootings and kidnappings – they all happened somewhere else, mostly north of the border (which was only ten miles away). But we were happy in our neutrality and in our ignorance. We would not be part of anything that had the word 'trouble' in it. We never did anything wrong ... or right. We were just mice in a ditch.

But the Don Tidey story continued. He had been taking his 13-year-old daughter to school when his car was stopped and he was abducted. His son and

daughter were left by the side of the road while the kidnappers brought him on a tour of the country. No one
knew where he was. The kidnappers were asking for
five million pounds sterling. 'That's a sight of money,'
my father said. He was right – because no one talked
in millions back then except Kojak and ministers for
finance and kidnappers.

The year 1983 was a runt of a year for me: lots of
promise, but no growth. I had played Minor, Under-21,
Junior and Senior football for Leitrim that year, and I was
as well out in Drumshangore Bog. Or so the Auld Lad
said. I was as proud as punch to play for the Senior team,
while still a Minor. So proud to tog out with the likes
of Micky Martin, Frank Holahan, Dan Meehan, Micky
Quinn and my own clubman, Seamie Mac. These were my
idols … and there were moments of great hope. There's
that word again: *hope*. Hope, me foot. We ran Galway to
a few points in the Minor and Senior championship and
that was it. That was the great saying in Leitrim at the
time: 'We ran them to a few points.' I was sick of running
everyone to a few points! And then, when the intense
football season was over, we had the hay and the bog and
the stubbing whins and this new bloody house. A frigacy
of a thing if ever there was one! We had dug out the foundations when I was sixteen! Did the Auld Pair want to

pay off the council loan before we moved in? Christmas was mentioned as a possible moving date. Moving? We were only moving 60 feet forward into the field ... but 60 feet was a lot of movement for our family. There would have to be Masses said ... and there was.

Then, on the 14th of December 1983, our quiet little world was turned upside down. First, Mammy saw a car with flashing blue lights going up the road. Apart from the sight of visitors, that was the worst thing you could see at the time – the sight of Guards.

'What's going on? Where are they going?' A few 'Jesus, Mary and Joseph's and we were into Armageddon Wednesday. It was early morning, the cows were milked, me and Mammy had to go to work. But would there be a house to come back to? Because now there were squad cars and army vehicles heading up and down the road and over by Aghavilla and out from Carrigallen. And 'Jesus, Mary and Joseph' again. 'What the frig is going on? We'll all be dead in the morning ... Jesus, Mary and Joseph.' But, at least, no one had gone off with the top of the milk.

The Auld Lad was having his tea before he went to the creamery. He took up his usual position at the table in under the radio and the Sacred Heart lamp. The radio was on, as it usually was ... the constant drone of news making no odds to us in any way, shape or form. Unemployment was widespread ... yet we hadn't time to do the things. Emigration was rampant ... yet we had no place to go. Bombs and shootings at every dawn, and yet we continued to ignore the outside world at every opportunity. We were as lucky and as passive as any one family could be. Daddy blew his tea, sipped his tea and sliced the top of his egg ... all without disturbing his neutrality. He put a lump of butter on his egg to permeate his intent, and indeed, could have been to the creamery and back without thought nor care if it hadn't been for the bloody news.

The radio was reporting on the Don Tidey saga. 'Reports are coming in ...' it said, and then Mammy came running in.

'That lad that was kidnapped above in Dublin is now beyond in Ballinamore or outside Ballinamore ... in a wood or a forest or a drain ... and there's Guards and army jeeps going up and down by here, and ... Jesus, Mary and Joseph ... what if they look up and see the state of this place? What's going to become of us?'

The Auld Lad was caught in the crossfire of conjecture between Mammy and the radio. The radio firing out facts and Mammy firing out fears. Daddy nearly didn't eat his egg with the rudeness of the interruption, but he did. And after he ate his egg and drank his tea and washed his cup, he said, 'I better go to the creamery or they'll be looking for me too.' Which made no sense whatsoever, and he knew it didn't. But his motto in times of strife was always: Keep Continuing.

My father was a bright man ... a shrewd operator ... always thinking beyond point. But a man so comfortable in his own mind that he'd nearly forget to suck his own sweet. He was always calm. Even amidst the current mayhem, my father had found a way to go slow. And although attempts were being made to jolt him into action – for him to take on a leadership role in our fight against terrorism – with my mother plucking names of saints from every corner in an attempt to highlight the immense danger that was abroad in Ballinamore and the potential threat of gunfire and visitors, it was my father's decision to stay chilled till it was over. We would continue moving forward at his own pace ... mesmerising army, Guards, Church and State in the process. My father would not be put out by anyone.

He left the high frequency of our old kitchen, put the trailer on the car, put the milk cans in the trailer and went off to Killegar creamery ... like he did every second day of the week and every second weekend of the year. Mammy fired an extra 'Jesus, Mary and Joseph' after him, but he never looked back. He needed no saints or members of the Trinity to ride along.

By lunchtime, word had filtered through that there were army and Garda checkpoints everywhere. Everyone was under suspicion, and according to my mother, under threat. The words 'Leitrim' or even the 'north-west' had rarely adorned our radios or televisions, and yet here we were, right in the nation's eye ... and for all the wrong reasons! There was an excitement about it. Excitement and rumour all around us. We had been preparing for Christmas and moving into our new house, and now there was talk of no Christmas or going out or carrying on. What would become of us all?

By the evening of the 14th of December, we knew exactly what was going on. Pat Fitch had arrived with an update at 11 a.m., and then every hour on the hour after that. And, although we all had phones by then, Pat preferred to deliver the news in person. Just as he did the death notices every morning after he read the daily paper. Don Tidey was being held captive in a place called Derrada in Corraleehan, only four miles from Ballinamore. Pat had counted 24 squad cars going up our road so far today. He wasn't sure if they were all different squad cars, but that's what he counted. And 18 army jeeps – and all carrying guns!

'There's a checkpoint at the mart. Another at Corrawallen, and Jercyful Maysus, another at Drumcoura.
All pointing guns here, there and everywhere. I didn't
venture any further in case I'd be taken in and shot dead.
But feck me, there must be quare skullduggery going
on with the whole army and Guards on high alert and
atein' nothing only bags of chips.'

Pat wanted to make sense of it. We all wanted to
make sense of it. To be part of it ... and yet remain
not affected by it. We tried desperately to find a reason
to go out into it ... to experience the trappings of kidnapping. Of course, at the heart of it, there was fear
and danger and ultimately death. A young Garda
and a young soldier were killed in exchanges as Don
Tidey was finally rescued on the following day, Friday,
the 16th of December 1983. But we, the youngsters of
the time, made every excuse to go places; to be stopped
and questioned by young, frightened men, not much
older than ourselves. We were so desperate to be part
of something – to be in the middle of the chaos and the
mystery and the terror. In fact, the tension and the terror
for those few days was so much that when it came to an
end on the Saturday morning, we found it hard to come
down from the high of it all and return to our usual low:
our normal, quiet, mundane lives.

On the following day, Sunday, the 18th of December 1983, with Christmas before us and the Tidey kidnapping behind us, we moved into our new house. My youngest sister, Geraldine, grabbed a few blankets and said, 'I'm moving.' And that was it. She did and we all followed. All of a sudden, we were watching *Glenroe* in our swanky new sitting room with radiators on the wall and a bathroom down the hall. And it was ... odd. We were no longer the family without a bathroom; the family who had to empty the pisspots and fill the tank and chase the American twin-tub washing machine down the street. We were now normal. And that didn't seem right.

One-way

May Quinn sat with her prayer book and a bush-full of hair on the back of her brother's Ferguson 20 TVO tractor. They were chugging along the Drumeela road on Sunday, the 25th of December 1983. It was Christmas morning, and they were heading to ten o'clock Mass. They were early. So was I. I was caught behind them. You could never get by the Quinns – Michael wasn't one for pulling in. May was his wing mirror. She sat facing the rear, relaying to her brother the length of tailback on the Drumeela road. Not that it made any difference – he still wasn't pulling in. This morning the Drumeela road was one-way. The Quinns were going to Mass.

May Quinn waved when I first crept up behind them; a big happy wave – a wave for both of them! We couldn't have been more contrasting. Me, full of the woes of being an overgrown 18-year-old. My youth had been one prolonged nappy rash. My family was an ever-evolving embarrassment, and my love life was devoid of love, sex and sexual know-how. On the other hand, May and Michael Quinn were just two well-worn Catholics on the way to remould their souls.

I don't know when I eased off on religion. I – like most of my generation – was brought up on Catholicism. Brought up to believe, to know, to *trust* that God was there ... and that he was watching and listening and tut-tutting at every opportunity. When I was younger, I was fully into God and religion and felt safe because of my belief. Everything I did was because of God and his Mother and all those saints that Mammy used to call on when there were visitors coming up the lane. And then in my teens, I started to slip ... only using God when I needed him. I'd pray like anything when there was a big football match coming up. 'Dear God, help us beat Drumreilly.' Or if I couldn't sleep, I'd pray instead of counting sheep. God was just the boy when you couldn't sleep – or when we were playing Drumreilly. But then there were the times when I was courting in the car and God would stick his head up from behind the seat and say, 'What are ya at there, young fella?' That's when you start to form differ-ent opinions on God and all that is good. How come everything satisfying is either ungodly or has too many calories? For now, the best place for God was over in the chapel, and the best time to visit was on his son's birthday at Christmas.

I have always loved Christmas. Yes, the indulgence of it – but also the essence of it. The Church does Christmas well. We had been to midnight Mass the night before, a time when midnight Mass was at midnight. And midnight Mass was always special. The excitement of being up so late ... going to Mass in the dark ... the chapel decorated to the last ... the lovely hymns and the procession of new coats going up to Communion. Obviously, everyone with a new coat had opened their presents early. Not much point having a new coat, if you couldn't swagger up the aisle giving it a bit of air. It was like a fashion parade in Drumeela every Christmas. And these weren't coats out of Mullen market. These were real expensive yokes out of the many local boutiques that had shot up in our towns and villages in the 1980s. Lovely little shops full of lovely dear things that no one could afford, except at Christmas or for a family wedding.

'You wouldn't be long getting rid of the creamery cheque in Rachel's Boutique,' according to Pat Fitch. How Pat knew that was a mystery, seeing as Pat wasn't exactly one for buying the mother a fancy coat in Rachel's Boutique.

May and Michael Quinn hadn't been to midnight Mass; the Twenty tractor was never taken out after dark – driving at night with the headlamps on would only waste good battery. So, ten o'clock Mass on Christmas morning was their time to shine. May didn't have a Christmas coat; she had 20 coats – and not one boutique disturbed in their acquisition. She was a bundle of thrift: coats and garments, patched and reinvented. An ensemble of colour to keep her warm and protected and anchored to her throne. She was a tiny little bird of a woman with a gallivanting head of hair. Only for the coats, she'd have been blown away, so my mother would say. Michael, on the other hand, had doom and gloom to weigh him down. That, and a hat and a brown pinstripe suit.

I was on a mission that morning. I was one disgruntled Christian crawling behind the Quinns. I needed to talk to God. I had talked to God in the past, talked to him when I was a boy. This morning, I would talk to him man to man – he was going to get some grilling this morning. This would be fightin' talk. God needed to change his ways. I didn't want God popping up at inopportune moments in my life, tut-tutting and wagging his finger when I was up to no good with a young one. A young man has to do what a young man has to do.

I wasn't sure what a young man had to do, but surely, it wasn't always watching out for God? This was the start of the new me ... grown-up me ... independent me. The me that was on my way to Drumeela to talk to an invisible man who has never been seen in Drumeela or anywhere else. And the other thing was, I was still behind the Quinns.

Maybe I was stuck here for a reason: to analyse human life in its most basic form – the Quinns. The Quinns never did any harm; farmed all their lives; said their prayers; went to Mass; paid their dues. They lived in Aghavilla House – named so to give it gravitas and importance. May longed for importance. She bossed her brother and polished his wellingtons every Sunday and holy days. Only on Christmas Day and for funerals did Michael wear shoes. He milked cows and sent milk to the creamery. He smoked Woodbine cigarettes in instalments. Three smokes out of every fag. That was the Quinns. No swimming pool. No sex orgies. No pulling in to let people by.

And I didn't want swimming pools either ... or sex orgies. I'd probably end up holding someone's coat at a sex orgy or going for a rope. But, surely, there was more to this world ... more to this life? As yet, I hadn't found it.

Eventually, we arrived at Drumeela and it was still early. The Quinns dismounted and went in the Drumbrick end. I parked and waited.

There was no frost that morning – no perfect backdrop to a Christmas scene. But neither was there rain or wind; just a few townlands silently mapping out my view: Drumeela, Annagh, Drumbrick, Corglass and beyond. There was nothing to see here ... nothing to declare. The leaning telephone poles along the Carrigallen road; the pasty winter fields dormant and pale ... the trees hunched and subdued and holding on. Jim McCartin's cattle were pulling from a backload of hay left out at first light. The night, and the lights from the candles and the Christmas trees, quenched as morning came, sombre and new ... it was just another day.

Another day. What some wouldn't give for one of them. There was a graveyard full of ones who would love to be standing at the chapel gate or going into Kate Dolan's shop. To listen to the sound of cars arriving ... the opening and closing of car doors ... the 'Good morning's and 'Happy Christmas'es to one and all. To be going into Mass ... the children giggling and old men exhaling with excitement. What the ones in the graveyard wouldn't give for a sore finger or a bad knee or the chance to run and play ... let alone play for their county. How dare I scorn my lot and cast such big notions through such narrow sight? I was wrong again. Would I ever get it right?

After Mass, I went home alone. My mother and father and brother and my two sisters stayed and chatted for a while. I was beyond that; plus I had to let everyone see me spraying gravel around the car park as I took off. I was at home before the dust settled. I went into the new house. The fire was on. The Christmas smells were there ... but it wasn't the same. I went outside and across to the old house, the house we had vacated only a week before. It was cold, the old Rayburn mute; the press with open doors. The jam and the red sauce and the salad cream had disappeared ... only the Sacred Heart lamp stayed. Our old house was full of empty. We had moved only 60 yards, and yet, we had lost so much along the way. Or at least I had ... or thought I had. I was in no man's land! A young man with no land, no education, no pot of gold. All I had was a red car and a head full of me-me-me ... and I didn't like me. I hadn't started cursing yet, but I was beginning to think that 'me' was a bit of a bollix.

The rest of them came home then and went into the new house. Someone put on the kettle ... and lo, it boiled! A kettle boils anywhere. And suddenly the house was full of cups clattering and voices chattering about what went on at Mass, and who was there, and who had a new coat, and the state of May Quinn's hair, and who was home and who got engaged. We sat at the table and had tea and stole lumps of cooked ham from the 'good' Christmas ham and lathered butter onto white bread and got out the mustard and yet the penny never dropped – that this was a life full of riches and family and treasure. It was hardly going to dawn on me, and me eighteen, that this was a wonderful life. That this was a wonderful family. That this Auld Lad of mine was a wonderful Auld Lad and that I should be so grateful. How could I not think that? But I was too thick. There's nothing good about being eighteen … or nineteen, which was only round the corner. There was only one thing for my misery. To eat as much and as often as I could over Christmas and then see what happened in the spring.

The finger

I felt a strange sensation at the end of my right arm where my fingers and hand were attached. Not pain, but a loss of contact with a body part. Not good. I was in no position to be injured and the size of me – what would people say? I was playing for Leitrim against Galway in the 1984 Under-21 championship in Carrick-on-Shannon. A game that had a surreal feel to it from the start. There were no signs of greatness or promise coming through the Under-21 ranks at the time; interest was low and spectators were few and far between. One of those games that you didn't really think about – just turned up, put on the jersey and did your best. Sometimes these were the games where I would excel – games when I didn't think too much and just played. This evening, I was neither thinking or exceeding – just playing … and not playing very well. I was not alone, but when you're the 'Big Fella' you usually get the brunt of the slurs.

'Get out in front, ya big bollix.'

'Hey, Big Fella, will ya show for the fucking ball!'

At last, I was out in front, grabbed the ball and was half tackled – not a furious belt or a dirty stroke – someone put out a hand and caught mine, caught my finger and that was it. I passed the ball and went down on one knee. In *my* head this was a sign to the bench that the Big Fella needed attention. But the Leitrim medical team hadn't been formed back then – there was a lad with a bottle along the line, drinking most of it himself and paying little heed to big lads with sore fingers. I took off my glove and there peeping up at me was bare bone – the finger wasn't broken, merely pulled back so far it dislocated and prised itself out through the skin. Those close by winced and put their hands up to their heads. The lad with the bottle came running.

And still, I wasn't in pain; it just felt odd. And my first thought was: *I won't be able to work tomorrow.* My second thought: *I won't be able to play football for a while.* My third thought was: *Who is that eejit shouting?*

'Ya big sissy, O'Rourke. Will ya get up and play the game!'

Sport is funny like that – turns fairly decent humans into indecent twits. In my later years playing football, I enjoyed some of the well-crafted jibes from the side-lines, but at nineteen, they cut me to the bone.

The lad with the bottle said he'd have to bring me to the hospital, and he did. There was a hospital in Carrick – for the elderly and infirm – and that's where we went. The staff were slightly confused when this rather large young man arrived with blood dripping from his hand. Most of their patients were tiny, quiet, senile poor craturs, with all their limbs still attached. Here was a big sweaty galoot in overloaded football shorts with thighs the size of canoes and his finger hanging off. The Leitrim togs, matched by the overstretched number 14 Leitrim jersey, a monster of gigantic proportions; but inside, I was a harmless little boy who hadn't been to a hospital since my birth.

They set to work. They looked at my wound and said, 'Ya may go to Sligo with that.' The lad with the bottle sighed and said, 'That's the evening gone now.'

We headed to Sligo General Hospital and he handed me over to his medical colleagues and I was brought off to theatre and fixed. I eventually got fed – and a good job, because I could find my togs starting to slip. I'd lose weight horrid quick if I wasn't well fed. I was then told that I'd have to stay the night and I did.

I was put into a ward of auld lads … even aulder than my own Auld Lad. They surveyed me and took me in.

'Did ya only come in with the hand?'

'Jaysus, you're a big man.'

'And you come into the hospital with only a finger?'

'It must be broke in several places or you wouldn't be here.'

'It's not even broke the once …? Sure, they must have made a mistake.'

'Ya may go out and see if they'll let ya home.'

And then in turn, they started to snore and I welcomed the bulbous sound.

I welcomed the chance to rest: laying down my tired body and emptying my head. Apart from the snores, the ward was warm – a luxury I had only recently discovered. There was a bathroom … I was up to speed with them too. I now loved toilets which took both Ones and Twos. I still remembered the old days – which were only six months ago. Doing a Number Two in the pot under the bed in the old house was the cause of many a row – especially if it was fairly full to begin with. My brother, Kevin, would never be so lazy as to poo in a pot that was nearly full … but I would. The alternative was heading out in the dark and the cold and 'making your mess' in the outside loo. But that was all in the past.

I awoke in the morning, to find myself being examined, yet again, by a patient. 'You're a bloody big young fella. What age are ya?'

'Nineteen.'

'Are ya? You'll be twenty stone by the time you're twenty-one.'

That hit me like an iron bar. This man sounded like he knew what he was talking about.

He said, 'I'd know be the arse on ya that you'll just blow up like a balloon.'

And, of course, he was right. Old men back then, especially farmers, could size up an animal, or a man or a woman, in seconds. It's all to do with your metabolism and the structure of your bones, and judging by my big arse, this man could see a troubled road ahead. I was worried and thanked him for his advice. Twenty stone was the size of Mrs Boyle, or the egg man or Young Magee from Derrylin. That was not an affordable bulk for someone who had ambitions of athletic greatness. I couldn't wait to get out of the hospital to ... stop eating. They kept coming around with sups of tea and bits of bread and custard and jelly and you can't refuse that. You can't say no to strangers and them looking after you so well. The lad in the bed beside me – the lad who had predicted my fat future – smiling, enjoying the progression of my imminent obesity. Saying, 'In some countries, they'd cut off your arms, so that ya wouldn't be able to feed yourself.' I had grown a dislike for this man … and hospital life. Shortly after, the doctor told me to go home and come back in three weeks to get the stitches out.

My father and mother had picked up my car and clothes from the football pitch in Carrick. That's what parents do. They were desperate to get the keys of Tommy Reilly's workshop to someone of trust, so they could open up the following day. Our house had no concern for severed limbs or ill-health unless it was putting someone else out. It wouldn't matter if my mickey was hanging off, as long as Tommy Reilly wasn't annoyed or held up. A week was mentioned as adequate time off … not because my finger would be healed, but because arsing around for any more than a week was not an option.

The weather was good that week. The weather had been good all that summer, but I didn't like 1984. It was a year of change and coming to terms with my size and the size of what lay ahead. My dreams as a child had almost come to fruition. I hadn't dreamed of much: just to be this great footballer that everyone looked up to. And that my football prowess would lead me on to lead others – a kind of knight in shining armour, leading Leitrim to All-Irelands and donkey derbies and wellington throwing in the Olympics. Sometimes, my dreams

ran away with me. But there was always the Auld Lad
to bring me back to earth.

'What happened the finger?'

I explained.

'You mustn't have had much of a grip on the ball, or
that wouldn't have happened!'

He was right.

Some weeks later, on the hottest day of that scorching summer, I drove myself to Sligo to the hospital to
get the stiches out. I was seen straight away, and I was
delighted. They said they were bringing me into theatre
to remove the stiches. I thought that was odd, but, of
course, I didn't ask why. They gave me a paper gown
and some plastic covers for my feet and head. Everything
else had to come off – of course it did. The gown didn't
fit – I burst several holes in it on my first entry. A larger
gown was sent for, and I was told the opening goes to
the back. When my considerable arse was taken into
consideration, I was advised to put a second gown on
back to front, as I would be waiting in the public waiting
room and bare arses were not part of the culture in Sligo
General Hospital. I put on my flimsy plastic shoes and
hat and shuffled off to the public waiting area and sat
on the leatherette seat among the fully clothed. It was
still only 8 a.m. Still time to get in and out and be home

in no time. The sun came around the corner to say hello and decided to stay with me a while. After ten minutes, my plastic shoes had fogged up. My shower cap – the lid on this boiling pot – began to steam as a bead of sweat trickled down my face. The Big Fella was getting warm. The people around me were called one by one ... but naked, burly me, in my paper gowns and hothouse shoes, remained.

Time passed slowly – the temperature was 25 degrees and rising. I was 15 stone 9 and waiting. I sat for an hour, then two ... then four. Why were they doing this to me? And then I heard, 'Mr O'Rourke.' I hesitated. My head was wet, my feet were wet, and I was sitting in a pool of sweat. When I extracted myself from the leatherette seat, I left the two cheeks of my paper mâché suit behind, and I walked slowly down the hall, showing off to everyone my extremely large and scalded bum.

Land

I bought a bike in the North – a racer with ten gears and turned-down handlebars. The cat's meow of a bike. Got it cheap in Enniskillen, rubbed a bit of dirt on it and rode it through the customs the far side of Swad (Swanlinbar) and across the border. We were well used to smuggling our essentials across the border: petrol, butter, toilet rolls and an assortment of useless items that we bought just so we'd have something to smuggle. Driving through a customs check point with nothing to declare is one thing. Driving through customs with all sorts of shite and declaring nothing is a lot more fun.

I already had a bike – according to my father. *His* bike that I rode to Tommy Reilly's of the Rough Hill when I started work there at fifteen. A big, black, man's bike, but not a bike for fitness and recovery. After the finger, I had snapped a muscle in my thigh. I had felt a strain for weeks but kept playing till I could play no more. Back to Sligo hospital and they told me to stop playing football and just do some light work on the bike. I presumed they didn't mean my father's bike from the First World War. Besides, I was mad for a bike with turned-down handles. I wanted to emulate Sean Kelly and Stephen Roche. They were Irish cycling heroes. Cycling was Ireland's number one sport at the time. I wasn't going to add to that mantle ... but I could outride most tractors and some cars. We had any amount of slow, cautious, dangerous drivers down our way. Most of them got a licence without doing a driving test.

My father never did a driving test, but thought he was Sterling Moss. Because he was a renowned handyman and cut the neighbours' hair, he thought he was also king of the road – especially in snow. He thought he had a gift when it came to driving in snow. He hadn't. He was the only one locally who would chance driving in snow – that's all. Which meant he never ran into other road users. But he was adamant that he could avoid the skids like no other – that he was the Stephen Roche of driving in snow.

I took my cycling seriously. I bought a water bottle and never left the house without a chocolate bar in my shorts. I could imagine myself in the Tour de France as I went up the Toome Road – head down and mind the bushes. Yes, cycling was popular back then, but only on television or in the developed world. Down our way 'cycling for no reason' was mostly frowned upon – it was not essential. Certainly no one would be so foolish as to tog out like nowadays and wear helmets and padding in their Lycra shorts and then cheekily hold up traffic or cause lengthy delays at the coffee machine in Centra. All those riding bikes back then were either going somewhere important or just gone in the head. If I had stuck to the Newtowngore road or gone towards Carrigallen or Drumeela, I would have been okay. My own people would have no problem with one of their own cycling for no reason. Frank Mac or Edmond Patterson or Johnny Dolan would be delighted to see Young Rourke riding around on his bike. But heading up the Toome Road – peddling like billy-o into Drumreilly – was just downright bold.

'What's yer man doing on the bike?'

'He must have nothing else to do.'

'The greatest sign of a gobshite is to see a lad riding a bike and him with a car at home.'

'There was always a softness in them O'Rourkes.'

'Gone astray in the head since they built the new house ...'

And so the comments descended – in my head. But they're the comments you'd expect from them ones.

I only went as far as Pat Conefrey's, just before Hyland's shop at Corrawallen, then I turned back with the fall of the hill for Carrigallen. The voices in my head eased as I passed John Maguire's. I had to get back to where the air was familiar and breathable. But first I had to stop to look at cattle in Drumconlevan. We had cattle on my mother's uncle's land. His name was Michael Galligan, but he was dead, and although it wasn't our land, we had cattle there for a short time, and I had to count them. *One, two, three, four, five, six, seven, eight ... and the other one must be behind a tree or bush. That would be the nine. No point going across the fields for a closer look. But what if she's not there?* I had no interest in land or cattle or traipsing across fields of rushes and cow tracks ... but today, I better double-check, as it was the only farming-related thing I had to do or intended doing for a while.

I wasn't a farmer, but a farmer's son. The land did not call me or my sisters as it did my brother. Good job it didn't. There was hardly enough land to make one of us miserable, let alone divide the misery into four. But land was everything ... to some. I left my bike at the road and walked across the barren valley to my grand-uncle's farm. He had looked after it in life as he now did in death – letting nature do her thing. And nature wasn't busy there that day. The farm had a worn-out look like the knitted auburn cardigan that my mother knitted for my First Holy Communion in 1973. An Aran cardigan crafted with love and frugality. A cardigan the colour of Drumconlevan on that late August evening, with the sun unseen and the clouds morphing into trees and bushes and unambitious grass. I walked past the tiny cottage where the departed man once stood; where he guarded against the gloom and the torment of time with nothing audible or awful to say.

I have nothing against land. After all, it is the earth that feeds us and that we return to when we're done. But I have no *grá* for land that consumes us, divides us, sucks the life out of us. Land that was never ours to begin with. In this country, we have a natural longing for what was once taken away from us. Some would do anything to obtain it. Some died trying to hold on to it. Many's a family was ruined by having it. I preferred to leave it to my father and my brother, and I would cycle around it, or one day write about it, but I have no hankering for land. No, sir.

The cattle were all there, all nine of them, and not a cud to chew between them. They might as well have been on an airport runway for all the nutrients they could find here. Indeed, like the Irish youth at the time:

the airport runway threw up more prospects than the stagnant country left behind.

Emigration was rife back then and going abroad had been whispered everywhere I went. I looked to the cloudy skies that day, and for the first time, thought about going away. London or England had never been on my radar; Australia was on no one's radar. Canada or exotic lands – no. But America was there. My aunts and uncle were there – especially my uncle Michael. He brought stories of great colour, and sun, and two televisions per house instead of only one. For the first time in my young life, I imagined myself somewhere other than Leitrim or Carrigallen. My only thought was for this football career of mine – a career that may have been past its peak. I didn't think of my parents; they would always be there. I had no friends ... that I could think of. My sisters were grand; my brother had the land. I was a perfect candidate for going abroad and making my fortune. I was a carpenter. I was as strong as an ox and thick as a mule ... I had no education to hold me back ... no girlfriends or secret lovers. In fact, my life was fairly shit all round. I had done nothing worth holding on to. Then I entered all my wows and whoas into an equation – without calling on the word 'hope' – and what came out the other side was a bit ... scary. Was this emigration I could see staring me in the face?

I got back to my bike and rode home like the bejaysus. I had intended on going for a 10-mile cycle after I had looked at the cattle ... cycling around the roads like the county man that I was ... working his arse off to get back to what he did best: being a supreme athlete and single-handedly carrying my county to glory or freedom or wherever had the most 'Good man yourself's in it. But all that was nonsense. I couldn't carry a county. I couldn't even carry a chocolate bar in me shorts without it running down me leg. I wasn't a hero or even the makings of a hero. I was Seamus Patrick Billy-no-friends O'Rourke. I was nineteen and full of my own delusion.

My father asked did I look at the cattle and I said I did – that was usually the length of conversations in our house. I wanted him to ask me another question or even make some sideways remark about my new racer bike. I wanted to know what was keeping me here in this place. Was it my parents? I wanted my father to talk to me ... to find comfort in the sound of his voice. But my father always said what he had to say without saying much.

So, I said, 'That's not great land about Drumconlevan.'

And he said, 'No, it's not. It's much the same as the land around here ... only it's over there.'

Aye, good man, Daddy ... don't get into a conversation whatever ya do!

My mother appeared. 'Did ya look at the cattle?'

'I did.'

'Were they all there?'

'They were.'

'Are they all still alive?'

'I think so.'

The Auld Lad said. 'Mmmmm ...'

That was it. I was halfway to the airport after that. I had fed off my parents long enough. They had nothing left to give, except swap words with no meaning or flavour, and it wasn't their fault. But I wish they had told me sooner that I was fully grown. That it was time I was taking flight. I wasn't ready to go anywhere, and God only knew where I might land.

Speak now

I unlocked the door of the old Protestant school in Newtowngore. Suddenly, I was hit with an unmerciful smell – the smell of smelly feet. We used to use the lovely old school for our local Macra na Feirme club. Supposedly a young farmers' club, but our Macra had all sorts, including farmers. Although it was based in Newtowngore, it was called the Drumeela Macra na Feirme. Its members, including myself, had been doing our first karate class there the night before. Karate was new to us and involved removing your shoes and socks. This didn't cause too much concern at the time, but having spent the night swirling around the old classroom in the dark, the juices from the young farmers' feet had fermented and ignited a pong of atomic proportions. We did a lot of things well in our local Macra club … perhaps karate wasn't going to be one of them.

Having spent a good stretch of 1984 on the sidelines with dislocated fingers, pulled muscles and faltering sprits,

I was at a loss for something to do. Yes, I was thinking of going away ... but I was also thinking of joining the army or the priesthood or becoming a pilot. Anywhere that I didn't have to come up with my own tune – where I could just sing along. I found being nineteen was a bit like when I was learning to ride a bike. I was fine if I rode in straight lines ... but changing direction was difficult and the prospect of coming off was frightening.

I think it was James Lee who said to me, 'Would you think of joining the Macra? It's fierce craic and there's women and everything.'

I wasn't sure what the craic was or what the 'everything' was ... but he had me at 'women', and I said I'd go. I hadn't had much involvement in clubs other than a football club. The football club, as a youngster, was easy. You togged out and you played. This was a club that sat. I had joined the Pioneers for a while after my Confirmation. There's nothing wrong with people who vow not to drink, but the ones who join the Pioneers would drive you to drink. I had also been to a few football AGMs. Another reason to have my doubts.

I didn't know what to expect when I sauntered into my first Macra meeting, but I knew enough to leave my big football ego at the door. I couldn't get over the amount of people – over 30 young locals; youngsters

I had forgotten about. I had left school at fifteen and worked for a man who employed only three others. I didn't drink, so I was hardly ever in the pub. And the only others I engaged with were footballers and ones going to Mass. This social gathering was a novelty, if nothing else. And because I wasn't expecting much ... I was surprised. There was lots of good humour and noise and then Michael McGovern called the room to order. He was the chairman and Pat Mitchell was the secretary. The room fell into silence. Pat Mitchell read the minutes of the last meeting and I couldn't believe my ears. This crowd of local young ones were organising ploughing matches and sports days and summer festivals. They were taking part in talent competitions, farm walks and a plethora of events and outings including discos, tractor reversing and duck racing. And although I wasn't into all of them, I realised that there were a load of things happening outside of my world, and just because my world was crumbling in and around me, it didn't mean that the world was ending or that God was picking on me by giving me this big arse and the enormous weight that I was carrying around on my shoulders. Maybe there was more to life. And no, I didn't say anything out loud or partake in any discussions, but I did admire them – all of them. We were in an old schoolhouse, there was no bar or beer or band – just ideas and opinions and organisation; and it was free and freeing and fun, and I was definitely coming back. I wanted more of this.

Young people getting up and speaking their mind – or just speaking in front of the room – was completely alien to me. I had heard people speak in public before. The priest at Mass, usually with a voice full of false rhythmic bounce, freewheeling through unconvincing tales. I had heard the politicians before an election, standing across the road from the church, pushing more unconvincing spiel. But they tended to bark, or drive their opinions hard, knowing their policies might not stand up to scrutiny if they dilly-dallied with their song. And then there were the football managers with their passionate calls for greater endeavour – roaring in metaphoric tongues:

'Stick to him like shit to a blanket.'

'Put your head where you wouldn't put your hand.'

Or 'Man and ball ... fuckin' man and ball!'

Not many public speakers had grabbed my attention like Dr Martin Luther King or John F. Kennedy. Or even our own Joe McCartin, who was a member of the European Parliament at the time. A man that always got his point across. Whether you agreed or not, he spoke with an articulation that was hard found down our way back then.

Of course, I never saw myself standing before the throng ... I didn't have anything to say. I would not want the eyes of the room falling on me. I was shallow and shy and had little interest in anything other than following the leader or simply staying put. But that changed at the next Macra meeting. We gathered the following Wednesday night; there was once again the same buzz and energy. I knew everyone there – some better than others. Pat Mitchell was a good friend of mine; only a few months younger than me, blessed with an enthusiasm and positivity that I certainly didn't possess, and a rogue and three-quarters to boot. The meeting started and the minutes read and the agenda dealt with, with gusto. At some point, Pat Mitchell was giving his view on certain topics, and somehow managed to bring it around to me. Probably an afterthought to get me involved. First of all, he praised me to within an inch of my big red face exploding. Then he asked for my opinion on what was up for discussion.

'Karate, Seamus. You're a top-class athlete, what would you think are the benefits of karate?'

I was up. I thought I would crumble ... melt in the eyes of the glow ... what else would a buck-eejit do? But instead of wilting, I grew. I knew nothing about karate, but from the moment I was given my cue, I felt empowered. Thirty or so young people were waiting for me to speak. For the first time in my life, I felt a power that I had never held before. I was not the victim of their stare, but the holder of their attention. I hadn't a clue what I was talking about, but they listened, and when I made them laugh, they listened even more, and I grew in confidence. No, I was not nervous. I was filled with a potent energy ... I had found some kind of crock of gold.

The maturity of these young people at the time was remarkable. They delighted in problem-solving. Where others would dwell in the negative, the Drumeela Macra na Feirme gang would build bridges and dams ... reach out and across the community and draw everyone together to make their place a better place. A training I never expected and will never forget. I would become the chairman of our club in years to come, take my first feeble steps into acting on a Macra na Feirme stage and learn the art of head-banging from some of the best head-bangers ever to put on a pair of wellingtons.

We organised the Leitrim ploughing match that year in Cathal Farrelly's field in Carrigallen. It was held on Easter Saturday, the 21st of April 1984, and the following day our new GAA football pitch was officially opened just out from the town. I played two games that day – a club game against Tara GFC from London and a county game against Cavan and ... I don't remember either one. I do remember the Friday before – Good Friday – when our lovely neighbour Beesie Mimna died, and our house fell quiet and sad. Myself and Kevin helped dig her grave, and everyone talked about the scorching sun and the weather taking up, and my world had never been so full ... of life and death and earth and play. And I even squeezed in a bit of romance at the ploughing match dance. Who'd want to go away? Who'd want to leave this wonderful place? This oddball community that thrived on adversity ... where dancing and sporting and high-kicking were all the rage.

The karate nearly killed me. Whatever muscles it called on, I hadn't used them before. I was barely fit to get out of bed the next morning, and when I opened the school the following night, with the smell that would knock a horse, I had a rethink. As the new head of the Drumeela Macra na Feirme sports department, I suggested we take up swimming, or in the case of most, who couldn't swim, swimming lessons. At least we'd be somewhere where we could wash our feet and we'd get to see the girls togged out – what could possibly go wrong?

Many of us who were part of Drumeela Macra na Feirme's golden years eventually got dragged into the Corn Mill Theatre, or its forerunner, the Carrigallen Community Players. We had gained a certain amount of neck from standing up in front of our gatherings at the schoolhouse or making our point at a debate in some far-flung parish hall. Or maybe it was because we were fed up with karate and in-house discos and tractor reversing and guessing the weight of a cow. Or the fact that the school fell into disrepair, and we had to move our meetings to Gorby's Lounge. Nothing wrong with Gorby's Lounge – we were glad to get it at the time. But once the drink was there and available, Drumeela Macra na Feirme was never quite the same.

Kaliber and white

I approached the steps of Wharton's bus with an air of emptiness. I was heading off on a football weekend, but I wasn't going to be playing any football. I was injured again. A tournament in Kerry – four teams from four provinces. Carrigallen was representing Connacht, but due to lack of numbers prepared to travel on such an unnecessary excursion, we had borrowed a few players from Fenagh. Fenagh Gaelic Football club was from the far side of Ballinamore and the perfect match for us at the time. Far enough away to avoid bitter rivalry, but near enough to harbour friendships and the same lacklustre approach to our national game. This was a weekend for craic and devilment and the bus driver greeted us with a beaming big smile.

Wharton's Coaches were one of the very few companies providing a coach service at the time. But most of the time, they were carting ones off on pilgrimages to

Knock or Lough Derg. They had made a fortune bringing people to see the Pope in 1979 – holy water and
prayer books all over the aisles for a week. Pope John
Paul II – a rockstar of a pope – from the Vatican City to
the Phoenix Park, then to Galway, Limerick, Drogheda,
Maynooth, Knock and even Clonmacnoise. The Pope's
Irish tour was Top of the Pops and Wharton's Coaches
were boiling with delight. Their drivers wore halos
and matching sunglasses ... a full week of rosaries and
novenas and hymns down the back. And when these
drivers weren't on religious duties, they were taking ones
to bingo or school or on school tours – pure torture for
a promising alcoholic like the driver that greeted us this
morning outside the hall in Carrigallen.

We had just about gathered up enough players for
the long journey to Abbeydorney in County Kerry.
Although Abbeydorney was a Kerry club, it focused
mostly on hurling at the time and the reason for this
once-off tournament over the long weekend was to
promote football in the area. Hence the calling on two
half-clubs from south Leitrim. None of this made sense.
I couldn't play, I didn't drink, I was no fun to anyone,
and yet here I was with my weekend bag. A few pairs
of socks and jocks stuffed into my football bag – a football bag without football gear. I would go with the flow.

I wasn't going to add to proceedings, but maybe there was something I could take away.

The next few passengers arrived. Aiden Harte and Sean Donnelly. They were not players but would bring some colour and drama. In fact, Harte and Donnelly at the time could provide a whole menu of distraction to an uninflated spare tyre of a young fella like me. Sambo Reilly was late – a man to cause bluster everywhere he went. And PJ Maguire – our boisterous captain – leading us forward and astray. My sprit was rising along with the decibels, and we hadn't even taken off. There was a head count – enough to play a game and some left over to mind the bus. The driver checked his rear-view mirror and smiled once more, and then ... we were off!

Sean Donnelly was a conspicuous man, to say the least. He had a round, friendly face with long '70s rock 'n' roll hair and sideburns. Because of polio as a child, he walked with a limp – but there was nothing lame about Sean. As quick a wit and as resourceful a man as you could find. He was always 'on' – loved porter and big feeds. He could dismantle a barrister with a word and charm the birds from the trees.

What Sean missed, Aidan Harte would take up. Tall and thin, agile in mind and imagination – he was hooked on drink and Shakespeare, and always knowing a hawk from a sparrow. He too had charm. He would charm the nuns by day and empty the pub by night. He was a teacher in Loreto College, Cavan until three o'clock ... and then he'd slalom his way through every public house on his journey back to Carrigallen, always ending up in the Kilbrackan Arms Hotel, a hotel owned by his brother. There, he and Sean Donnelly would take each other on in a game of 'You're talking shite again', and 'Kiss-me-arse' and 'Lord, you're an awful bollix'. Indeed, it was always open season in Carrigallen for rare and wonderful species of humans like Donnelly and Harte. No wonder the Australian woman said that a visit to the Kilbrackan Arms of an evening was like walking onto the set of *One Flew Over the Cuckoo's Nest* – an ale house and a mad house like no other.

The weekend away started in the pub – I had no problem with that, no problem with my Kaliber and white – a concoction of alcohol-free beer and white lemonade. It didn't taste great, but it looked like a lager, and thus, I looked the part. I had spent many's a night in Gorby's Lounge after a Macra meeting drinking the stuff. A time when we went to the pub for the fun and the company, and the drink was coincidental. How long would that be the case? I was not a teetotaller for any particular reason, and I was neither determined to remain one nor to break into the world of drinking. But there were some claims that 'loosening up a bit' mightn't do me any harm. I was nineteen, and not drinking from here on in would need explanation or a medical certificate. And there were plenty others who didn't drink – Seamie Mac or my brother Kevin, Brian Doyle, Micky Lee and Michael Donohoe. There was no pressure on anyone to drink and that's the way it stayed.

The next day the lads won the semi-final. Great. They would play St Anne's of Dublin in the final. The highlight of the semi-final was the performance of Brian Doyle. Brian was a bit older than me. He was a fantastic footballer in need of a little confidence. The semi-final gave him that – he scored a bag full of goals and was justifiably on cloud nine – a few clouds up from where I was at the time. And it was such a relaxed weekend that we went back to the pub. The account of the day's exploits was given a coat of polish, and suddenly, this was one of the greatest triumphs known to man. The euphoria demanded more than Kaliber and white … for some. I hadn't played, and although delighted with the victory, my spirits were not rising to the occasion.

'Will we have a pint, Rourke?' a giddy Brian Doyle mouthed.

I said, 'You've a game tomorrow.'

'I know, that's why I need a pint … in case me energy drops!'

I was blasé.

'Come on, Rourke, we'll have a pint tonight, and then we'll always remember when we started drinking!'

He was right. I said okay. It was Kaliber and white no more. Doyle bought two pints of Harp, because of the way Sally O'Brien used to look at him on the television. That was it … we didn't horse into them, just drank them, and I got two more. Then Doyle went off to tell some young one about the three goals he had scored that day and then he scored again. He was on a great run of form, to be fair. I finished my pint and had another and that was it. Three pints of Harp and it didn't do anything for me. I left it at that for the night. It was going to take a lot more than three to get me going.

There are all sorts of tales from that famous trip to Abbeydorney in '84! Some about the heroic victory in the final against the Dubs; about Brian Doyle's man-of-the-match display and another bagful of goals. But most of the stories were about the drink and what went on because of the drink and that even O'Rourke was drinking and how could Doyle play so well after a bellyful of drink? Drink was now part of my life. And it wasn't a sudden demolition of all my principles and plans ... it took its time. I enjoyed the few pints ... but only in the same way as I had enjoyed the non-alcoholic brew. Harp wasn't nice ... I later switched to Guinness. Guinness wasn't nice either, but that was just the liquid. There was more in there ... much more.

Messrs Harte and Donnelly were never lacking when it came to performing under the influence. They got rat-arsed in Abbeydorney – the excitement of the sporting fair and the thin air of the south caught them by surprise. They were laid out in Wharton's bus for the journey home. Sambo led the prayers and after a short Mass, they started to come to in Granard. When we got back to Carrigallen, they leaked out of the bus and trickled off to their respective houses for beddy-byes.

Although we were backboned by the cream of the Fenagh club that weekend, the winning of the Abbeydorney tournament gave us all a lift and when our Under-21s, including myself and Doyle, played a month later with St Joseph's (an amalgamation with our neighbours Aughavas), we couldn't be stopped, and more silverware appeared. And celebrations ... and pints. And that was it – club football was over for the year.

The dark evenings of winter soon arrived, and I was summoned to help the Auld Lad in the shed.

'You wouldn't put a bit of weld on that – you'd be better at it nor me.'

Who was this man, firing out compliments like there's no tomorrow? We were making new gates out of upcycled rusty old ones – my father's favourite pastime.

'Do ya ever take a drink?' he said in between the sparks and the smoke.

'I do an odd time,' I said.

'A few drinks are nice, if you can leave it at a few,' he said as he chipped the flux off a weld. 'Some can't leave it at a few.' And then we had to turn the gate and get out the grinder and swap the cutting disc for a wire brush. And the work went on and he had had his say on drink.

My father liked a drink and delighted in being able to say, 'I have enough' – he enjoyed the power of control over it. And maybe I could weld better than my father, but not much else – he had a wisdom and grounding that I simply could never find.

Where is he?

Nineteen sounds young – but not when you're nineteen. I was coming up short on the football field. I played or trained or practised every day, and in the words of my father, 'I was as well-off peeling turnips.' When I wasn't playing – when I was injured – I did the only other thing I was any good at: I ate. Me and my brother could eat for Ireland. I had two fears. A fear of getting fat and a fear of not getting enough to eat. But I never thought I'd get too old to play football.

I once saw a grey bearded man tog out and take the field for a Senior football match in Carrick-on-Shannon. He was sixty if he was a day, or so I thought. I wondered why he bothered! There's only one time to play – when you're young and able to move. This 'auld fella' was part of the famous Allen Gaels club, a club based in Drumshanbo, and he turned out to be the match winner. He was light and quick and wicked as anything – plus, he had the wisdom of a Tibetan monk. I wished our team had an auld lad like him. A guiding light. A conductor. A beating heart. His name was Eamon McGowan and it turned out he wasn't as old as I thought. A man with a great career behind him; a man who was now the Leitrim Senior football manager.

As average as I was, I probably overachieved as a footballer. I wasn't athletic or built for high-performance sport, but in the winter of '84, I was back focused on playing again. I hadn't gone to the dogs with the pints of Harp. I was still on course to be something or somebody. And there was none of the self-doubting or feeling sorry for myself which usually tagged along in my world. And although my father had given me a great grounding in life – nailed my feet and every other part of my body firmly to the wet fields of Drumshangore – there were times when I nearly left the wellingtons behind me in the sodden gaps and began to rise. Times when I just got on with it; times when I didn't think too much and just played. This was one of those times. The reason for my new-found commitment was ... Eamon McGowan.

While plodding my way to Under-21 championship success with St Joseph's a few months earlier, I saw Eamon McGowan standing, watching from the side-lines. What could he be thinking?

Your man O'Rourke is woeful, and I hear he's drinking and thinking of going away. And he's always injured and he has some difficulty with his father. Sure, his father is a lovely tall man with a cap, and although he can't weld for shite, he's a man who deserves better from his son.

That's a lot of thinking and me in the middle of a big game ... but that's the way my brain worked – it had a mind of its own. At half-time in that final, Eamon McGowan came and walked off the pitch with me, and said, 'I think you'd make a great full back.' I had never played at that end of the pitch before – always at midfield or as a full forward. 'I think it would help your confidence if you were facing the ball for a change ... and with your fielding ability and your ability to read the game, I think we can find you a new home on the football field.' No one had ever used the word 'ability' twice in the same sentence while describing me before. I was transformed ... for the second half of that game and beyond.

For someone to believe in me ... was strange. And wonderful ... and I vowed to honour that belief and I didn't go mad drinking after the Under-21 final. I was still a 'three pints and I'm out' sort at that stage, but I kept my head down and focused. County training started back, and myself and Seamie Mac headed off every Tuesday and Thursday to Drumshanbo and did the simple winter training plan. Endless laps around the pitch, and then do it again! We'd take turns at the driving, and whoever was driving provided two apples for the journey home. Myself and Mac ate more apples that year and the craic was always good.

My father was fifty-seven and had just survived the building of an L-shaped bungalow – one of the most difficult architectural accomplishments since the pyramids. He had put up with a lot of change in his fifty-seven years and the last thing he needed was for me to switch positions on the football field. The wheel was round for a reason. The sun came up for a reason. The moon only came out at night – for a reason. There was no reason for me to start playing full back for Leitrim. It was the most irrational thing to happen since Micky Mac drank the burned engine oil.

Micky McAweeney was our neighbour from down the road – covered in carbuncles and grime. He used to get a bottle of milk from Tosh Rourke's for his tea. He had also asked Tosh for a drop of burned engine oil to rub on his bike before he put it away for the winter. One evening Micky got horrid drunk in Gorby's and stopped at Tosh's on the way home for the milk. Tosh's wife, Peggy, presented Micky with two bottles – one full of milk and one full of burned oil. Both wrapped in newspaper, both ready for the rocky journey home. When Micky woke in the middle of the night with a drought that would cause a small church-gate collection ... he downed the bottle of burned oil and still had milk for his tea in the morning.

'What are they doing, playing ya at full back?' my father said.

I said, 'They think I'll make a good full back.'

He didn't agree. 'They were as well putting in Micky McAweeney. Sure, you never played full back. It's the most ridiculous thing yet.'

The last bit got me. 'The most ridiculous thing yet.' What did he mean by 'yet'? In the history of mankind? It'll be on the nine o'clock news: *untalented Leitrim footballer moved to full back in an attempt to inflict even more embarrassment on his family!*

I went to the shed. The only thing I could do was ... to out-weld the hoor.

Our shed was a retreat – the place where the men of our house would go when there was upset or turmoil or confusion. A place full of inanimate objects: tools, yokes, bits and bobs. There was a bench inside the small side door at the window with a blacksmith's vice attached and a circular grinding stone ingeniously mounted onto a butter-churn winder. There was an anvil there. An arc welder plugged in at the big double doors at the front. Everywhere there was bits of my life … and my brother's life … and my father's life. The offcuts of the first trailer we made; the leftovers of old gates that we had transformed and given new life. The bits of two-inch angle where my father had learned to weld – childlike dribbles and spots of weld from his first attempts. I remembered patiently helping him at the time. He practised at every opportunity, and eventually, he came to me like a student to a teacher with a couple of two-inch flats welded together for life.

'Is that any better?' he said.

I said, 'That's it, you have it now!'

In the spring of '85 I was doing exams for my apprenticeship papers. I had originally thought that being a carpenter was just practical, but there was written work for the AnCO certificate and a City & Guilds cert that I had decided to do. I hadn't the luxury of doing my apprenticeship in college – I worked all through my four-year course, and now the exams would be done in my old vocational school in Carrigallen. I got up at 6 a.m. every morning to study. I was training harder for football than I ever had before. I was watching what

I ate … and I was in the shape of my life. I had new-found purpose, new-found drive … a new-found contentment with myself.

'Where's Daddy?' I asked one evening when I got home from work. Mammy hadn't gone to work that day, which was more than unusual. She was dressed up like she would be for a wedding or a funeral. 'Where is he?' I repeated.

'Your father's in the Surgical in Cavan.'

'Oh … What for?'

'They're doing tests. He might need an operation.'

'Oh … When will he know?'

'Tomorrow morning.'

'Oh. Is Kevin about?'

I had team news for the game against Mayo on Sunday. I was oblivious to any threat or danger to my father's health. He was always there – always continuing – always with something to say about the team for Sunday.

I was playing full back for Leitrim. We had squeezed past Sligo in a replay to get to the Connacht Senior semi-final. Mayo had former Offaly All-Ireland winner Sean Lowery playing at full forward – I was set to mark him. I wanted to see my father's reaction to that, but he wasn't there.

He had prostate cancer, and I should have been worried sick, but I wasn't. Firstly, because I didn't know it was cancer. Mammy never mentioned the big C word – just made loads of strange expressions with her mouth and eyes. Secondly, I was just gone twenty and I hadn't an emotional bone in my body. And thirdly ... I was going to be marking Sean Lowery on the 23rd of June 1985 in Carrick-on-Shannon. It was my mother's birthday, and Sean Lowery was a hero of mine, and now I was expected to hammer all kinds of shite out of Sean Lowery and my father wouldn't be there to see it.

I went to see my father after work on the Monday. He said, 'The match didn't go so well.'

'No.'

'Ah, Mayo would be very good.'

'They weren't that good.'

'There was a man here earlier, said today's paper gave you a good write-up. Said ya played well. If you could believe the paper ...'

My father was almost fully recovered from the operation and would soon be home. Of all the games I ever played, why was that the one he never got to see? Only to hear what the paper said ... if you could believe the paper.

Like a rock

In the summer of '85, I felt like the lad in Bob Seger's song, 'Like a Rock' – strong, bold and sweatin' in the sun. Except there was no summer sun in 1985. It was the first of the wet years – the next one being 1986. Apart from being as fit as ever I'd been in my whole life, and being only twenty years old and looking like I might actually make something of my lot, and the fact that my father wasn't going to die and that he almost said something positive about me in the hospital, it was still a desperate summer for hay. Rained the whole year. Ones ploshin' about in meadows trying to win hay, when winning hay was impossible. Winning hay that year was like Leitrim trying to beat Mayo or Galway in the championship – it was never going to happen. The farmers were in crisis. And not just Leitrim farmers. Farmers everywhere were crying out for sun or at least a day without rain. It didn't come. And the only alternative to making hay was silage. No one had ever heard of silage up to this point. How would we go about making that?

Silage is simple. Cut the grass in the meadow. Bring the grass into the silage pit. Stack it densely between two walls and then cover it and make it airtight with a plastic cover. No problem. That's what happens now. Now you don't even need the Auld Lassie to provide 20 dinners and 20 desserts per day for the fortnight of the silage. Now, the silage takes something like two days at most. But in 1985, when no one had harvesters or trailers or pits or walls or any experience of any kind other than flutin' about with hay for the best part of three months of the year, the easiest part of the silage was the 20 dinners and 20 desserts that Mammy would prepare in between working in the factory and milking the cows.

Making silage in 1985:

The tall farmer with the farmer's cap takes off cap and scratches head.

Tall farmer sends his youngest son down to the empty hayshed for a pitchfork and the grease gun and oil can.

Tall farmer puts an edge on the antiquated mowing machine – the mowing arm.

Tall farmer's eldest son puts an extra set of back wheels on the 135 tractor – 'double wheels' for those of a farming persuasion. Double wheels for the horrid wet meadows around the greater Drumshangore area.

With a wet and heavy heart, the tall farmer sets off to meadow number 1. Note: meadow number 1, better known as 'Grimes' meadow', consists of one-and-three-quarter Irish acres and is only accessible through a little prick of a gap that you'd hardly get a bicycle through, let alone a small tractor with double wheels.

Tall farmer abandons tractor and heads back to the yard for the digger. The digger is his beloved International digger – a contraption found only in poor countries where the word 'shame' is no longer in use.

Tall farmer, with great delight, gets the auld digger going and swaps the shoring bucket for the only other bucket available. Note: this bucket is known as the 'Other Bucket'.

Tall farmer slowly trundles off in the digger to meadow number 1.

Tall farmer widens the entrance gap to meadow number 1 in a matter of hours.

Tall farmer dismounts digger – has a piddle – and then reascends tractor and mower.

Tall farmer enters meadow number 1.

Tall farmer is called for the dinner.

After the big feed, the tall farmer reads the local papers: the *Leitrim Observer* and *The Anglo-Celt*.

Tall farmer returns to tractor and skilfully mows the grass – the double wheels keeping him afloat throughout.

There is now a change of machinery. The mower behind the tractor is replaced with the 'side-delivery' – that's what we called it. A yellow yoke with six pronged wheels which would normally caress hay into rows. But because there's no hay, the side-delivery rolls the long grass into a matted mess ready for the next part of the process.

Another change behind the tractor. We now introduce the buck rake. Normally used for lifting cocks of hay, it is now used to push the matted mess into piles, lift them and then head for the silage pit.

In 1985 the silage pit was strategically placed ... anywhere. Anywhere near the house, so that the men wouldn't have far to go for the dinner. There were no walls in these early silage pits. The pit would often rise to over ten feet at the high end. Buck-rake-full after buck-rake-full of entangled grass would be reversed up onto the pit and anything from four to twenty-four men would pounce on the pile with pitchforks and grape forks ... then grunt and fart and get in each other's way until the grass was finally distributed evenly around the pit.

Next, the rolling of the silage would commence. Because the grass needed to be compacted tightly together, some poor bastard of a young fella – preferably one of the tall farmer's sons – would carefully drive the tractor up and down the pit like a steam roller ... making sure to go as near to the edge and the end as possible. 'Near ones' and 'narrow escapes' were all the rage in 1985. Lads tumbling off silage pits was nearly an Olympic sport; as was getting stuck in wet meadows and gaps and pullin' and woolin' entangled grass and eating big dinners in the middle of the day.

That was the first meadow. There were ten more ... And, of course, the pit had to be covered – another week and more eejitin'. No one knew what they were doing, but they were doing their best.

'That's all anyone can do,' my father said. 'You can only do your best ...'

But what if our best isn't good enough? What then? That was my only concern as a 20-year-old. *Is what I'm doing good enough?* It didn't seem good enough for my father, although he never said that out loud ... but I was sure that's what he thought. But how could I be sure? I wasn't sure of anything.

'Are you going on this trip to America?' he asked. We were after a hard battle with silage that day – the arms nearly pulled off ourselves from it.

'I was thinking of going,' I said. The football club were off again, this time to America – New York, Hartford,

Connecticut and Boston. Going for a fortnight ... or that was the plan. Lots were thinking of a much longer stay. 'There's ones will probably stay,' I said.

He said, 'I suppose there is.'

Apart from that, he had no opinion. I waited for one, but no. My father had a knack of not saying much or saying nothing, whichever he felt would have the most impact. What he didn't say was always aimed at me.

His brother Michael went to America in 1958 and stayed. His sisters Monica, Theresa and Vera all went to America and stayed. His youngest brother, Kevin, was a missionary priest. He went to Africa and made a life for himself there and elsewhere. Only my father and his sister Peggy stayed in Ireland. Peggy was a nurse in Manorhamilton. Daddy was a tall farmer with a cap in the home place, and I often wondered did he ever think of an easier life in a country with less rain and no silage. Or what was it that had kept him here.

Maybe it was the rain? Duckin' in and out of the rain – the inclement weather part of the parameters to his farming life. The rain and the chance of rain along with the poor land had shaped him ... not allowing him to stride forward at a rate of knots, but to arm-wrestle with nature. To look nature in the eye ... to never forget that nature is everything.

And my father's affair with nature was far from love at first sight. I believe my father and the land were an enforced match. They had little in common, but they stayed together. His mother, my granny, had minded him like an egg, so that he would stay on the land. And now my mother, who cradled his very soul, needed him to stick to that plan. So from the moment he rises till it's time to go to bed, my Auld Lad – out of responsibility as much as love – is at one with the land.

When I was very small, I would sometimes be kept awake by a horrible thought that my father would not be there when I woke. That God would take him ... or the fairies ... or the wind. That I would not see his silhouette in the fields or in the byre or folding itself into the car. That when I'd walk past the window of the shed, that he wouldn't be in there footerin' and bangin' and making. Because my father was a maker, a transformer, constantly shaping and rearranging his tiny share of the world. He didn't let up till the morning he died in 2003 ... shook hands with my mother and said, 'I'm off, the best of luck.' Then he closed his eyes for the last time. He was gone. He didn't like cucumbers or three-quarter cups of tea. 'Fill it up ... fill it up,' he'd say. He never laughed at what English people thought was funny. He never joked unless he was in earnest, and he did not own a camera.

In the autumn of 1985, we sent our parents away on a trip to Kerry. It was their twenty-fifth wedding anniversary. It was also their first holiday since their honeymoon in 1960. We sent a Kodak Instant camera with them. They brought a camping stove with a small cylinder of gas with them in the boot to make tea. The Auld Lad lost his farmer's cap somewhere along the road, and when my mother forced him to go for a walk later that evening, he insisted on wearing a shower cap out of the B & B in case his head got cold. The next day they asked a stranger to take a photo of them by Lady's View near Killarney. My father – in his white Aran jumper that Mammy had knit and no cap. It was a great photo. The only photo. The other 24 photos on the camera were blank because Mammy had held the camera the wrong way round.

Changing colour

I'm like my father. I don't like holidays – going about looking at things and pretending you're interested is not for me. Or worse still, having to talk to people who love looking at things and insist on telling you about the things they've seen. I'd rather be in Drumshangore Bog. Going to America to play a few football matches and look at things wasn't doing it for me. In my football world, playing friendlies or tournament games in New York or London or some hurling part of Kerry had no street value. And maybe that sounds like I was a cranky bastard back then ...? Well, I wasn't. I just had my father's down-to-earth logic. Why go to America when we could stay at home?

We didn't have a full team prepared to go to New York, so ... over to the Fenagh boys again to see if they were interested. And they were. I got time off work – three weeks. I would have to do a lot of paying back on three weeks. Most young people heading off to America in the '80s had no intention of coming back. Most, disillusioned with their life in Ireland, wanted to get away from the rain and their parents, and the constant going to Mass, and having spuds and gravy with everything, and driving girlfriends around in cars and nowhere to pull in for a good court ... let alone anything else. Everyone wanted a bit of MTV America. Everyone had sexy busty babes from Baywatch swannin' up to them in their dreams or into a wet meadow and making them cry out for America. Our young farmers' mickeys were wrung out from watching *Baywatch* and *Wonder Woman* – they needed to go forth and sin for Ireland! And then there was the fellas coming back from America with their last 27 pay cheques still in their wallet – $800 and $958 – three million dollars an hour after taxes and a swimming pool! What were we doing working for £100 a week and bring your own sandwiches?

My brother Kevin was going to America ... a great experience for the two of us. Mammy made us buy lots of underwear because of the AIDS over there. The Auld Lad was losing his two best mules. We had made a few clunks of silage by then, but there were still meadows not cut, and we were now breaking into October.

'It's well for some,' he remarked as we headed off on that Thursday morning. No hugs or blessings, only,

'Make sure you give Uncle Michael that shirt.' Mammy had packed a horrible gaudy American shirt that he left after him when he was home last – probably left it behind on purpose – but we had to have something to give him.

'And get Margaret flowers or something when you get over.'

Margaret was our Uncle Michael's wife – a good tough Tipperary woman.

'She could probably manage without flowers,' my father said and I agreed.

We flew from Shannon. You could still smoke on aeroplanes in 1985 and I didn't know enough to sit in a non-smoking section. Anyway, the smokers were better craic. It was all new to me – exciting. I felt like I was going on a school tour with no packed lunch. And because we were going across water – the Atlantic – we got counted even more than we would on a trip down the country. We weren't as hard counted on the way back. Out of the 45 or so that left … less than 30 returned. A harmless football trip to America in 1985 had the potential to turn into an evacuation. '*Seamus is going to* A-MER-I-CA,' the young lads had sung a few days before. Now it was real.

For the previous year, I had coached the Under-12s – the kids. Some of them were less than ten years younger than me and we had a great time, because

I was still a kid too. They looked up to me – or so I thought. In hindsight, they probably thought that I was a bit harmless, but that I had a lovely shiny car. They were right on both counts. And back then I was on my own. No team of coaches and selectors and parents looking after an underage squad like now. No, I said I'd look after the Under-12s and that was what happened. I was there on my own every Saturday morning with a clatter of boys and girls, from six years up – talented, untalented … interested and not. Over-parenting and encouraging and encroaching were not yet born in the GAA. Most parents were delighted with the babysitting service. Some were annoyed that we took their babies away from their Saturday morning chores. But most didn't give a damn. Me and the kids got along grand, and the Saturday morning before I flew to New York, some of the Under-12s had gathered on the bonnet of my 'lovely' car and sang repeatedly as they bounced: '*Seamus is going to* A-MER-I-CA.'

John F. Kennedy International Airport was as bright as nothing we had seen before. God had used different crayons to colour here. We had left the watery grey skies of Leitrim for this eye-squinting dream world. Not a cloud to hang your coat on. Me and the brother, with our pale faces and suitcases full of underwear, standing in a gigantic bowl of blues and greens and yellows. And brown people everywhere. We're not in Drumeela now. Where was the uncle?

'Oh Jesus, there he is.' Daddy's brother, Uncle Michael, had the most American outfit on him as he approached – white trousers and big white runners. Sneakers. Hard to imagine our Auld Lad in that get-up. Daddy didn't even wear jeans. He wore suits – or what looked like suits. The good clothes that had got worn and torn and patched, then reintroduced as working clothes … now his official 'auld clothes'. Most things in our lives were recycled or reinvented or retained. Uncle Michael was like a butterfly that got dressed in a pound shop.

'Hey, welcome to New York!' Uncle Michael loved New York … but he mostly talked of Leitrim, the place he left over 27 years before. We got the big tight handshake then. Michael had a problem with loose handshakes, or slippery, soft ones like a priest. He'd grab your hand and squeeze. He liked being told that he had a great tight handshake. Of course, me and Kevin didn't take any notice. He could squeeze away at our hands – we were both blessed with big thick hands. Useful on a wet farm in Leitrim and now in New York too.

Where was the bus or the train or the big cars that the uncle was always talking about? The car was in the car park, and it was big – a horrid size of a yoke – and we were whisked away in the over-lit daylight to the Bronx.

Our Uncle Michael had an unmerciful *grá* for life. He was sixty at the time, forty years my senior, and he'd put ya to shame with his intoxicating energy and enthusiasm. Me and Kevin were steady-eddies: get up – eat – work – play football – go back to bed. Michael, according to himself, didn't really go to bed.

'Man …' He was up at 4 a.m. and doing his exercises and going for ten-mile cycles and two-mile runs and into the gym for sit-ups and pull-ups, and eating broccoli and then …

'Man …' He'd go to work in one of his bars – while interrupting burglaries and fighting crime and then …

'Man …' He'd go for another run, this time on one leg …

He was the chairman of the Leitrim People's Association and the Association of Leitrim People and the most Leitrim person in the St Patrick's Day parade and then …

'Man …' He'd go for a swim – up to Canada and back …

He was the furthest thing from his easy-going brother at home in Leitrim – who was just as proud of where he came from without the 3,000-mile cavity.

Michael and my father were opposites. The Auld Lad was tall – Michael not as tall as he thought. Michael had brains – my father had sense. Michael had tried everything – the Auld Lad was happy with what he had.

Michael drove us straight to his house. No time for buying flowers – not even time to get in a word.

'Welcome to the Bronx.' Michael's wife, Margaret, was as calm as you'd expect from a woman living with an active volcano. 'Don't mind Mike,' she said. And we didn't. Of course we didn't – we couldn't keep up with him – but we adored him. Here was this man who looked at the world and said, 'Wow!' *Wow* was not in our vocabulary. Being excited was not in our nature. In our world, a day where nothing went wrong was a good day … as good as it got. Now we were into 'Wow!'

We would stay with Michael and Margaret and their four kids for the New York leg of our trip, but there were games to play and a city to see and New York didn't disappoint. If ever a place looked like it did on the telly, it was New York. We were full-time looking up in the air … skyscrapers everywhere. 'How in the Lamb of Jaysus do they wash the windows?' That was one of the subjects up for discussion when the Carrigallen lads met in Rosie O'Grady's Bar on Seventh Avenue. The other one was – where would we get women? And then a warning about AIDS. But no one knew anything about AIDS or where you'd get AIDS. And was there any more chance of getting AIDS than there was of getting a woman?

And someone suggested that prostitutes were the only thing for short-term residents like ourselves. But that Irish lads had a tendency to not make the most of their allotted time with one of these ladies of the night … that sometimes, the cheese would be melted and it only in the oven. Seamie Mac said, if you named the Kerry team of '75 in your head, that this might prolong the procedure … but mixing football with sex didn't seem right. There was a fella from Ballyhaise in Cavan working behind the bar that evening, and he said that him and his mate had the same problem when they went to 42nd Street – got way too excited way too soon – so they started rubbing Bonjela on their lads before they went in. There was only one word for that – Wow!

Shovels McGrath

The women of New York were safe the week we were there – lots of brave and dirty talk, but no action. There were loads of social engagements and one-sided football matches against teams that seemed more concentrated on work the following day. I realised very quickly that, yes, there was good money to be made, but in America you earned it. It wasn't all drink and Bonjela – it was get up at 5.30 a.m. and work like a hoor. Most of our lads only greeted 5.30 a.m. on the way home. Of course, work and how America worked was on my radar. It was on everyone's radar. New York was the place to be in 1985 – out from the crime and the AIDS and the large numbers of Americans.

Our schedule brought us on to Connecticut, Hartford and New Haven, where we went fishing for bluefish in the ocean and nearly got drowned. Then to Boston and Harvard. It was the 'fall' over there – beautiful autumn colours and lashings of sun, like they had some left over from the summer. I thought of the Auld Lad at home, rubbing his knees together, waiting for a middlin' day to try and make hay. October hay was going to be a first in Ireland – even the worst farmers would have the hay got by September. But in 1985 things were different, and I was beginning to wonder if I would see home before the end of it.

Rumours were spreading that some of our foot-balling gang were staying on in the States. Some of the Cookes were staying; some of the lads from Fenagh. And Seamie Mac! Seamie Mac was a county man – a better county man than me with a family business at home. Sambo Reilly was staying; he had several girl-friends back home – what was he going to say to them?

'And what about you, Rourke?' they'd say. 'You're a carpenter, you'd make a fortune out here. Get your place on any team in New York, work hard, and come home in four or five years and build a house.'

I had enough of building houses … and I had a job with Tommy Reilly. Okay. I had no girlfriend, but a 20-year-old like me could fall in love between two showers of rain – if it would only stop raining. There was also my football career and my— Hold on! I was running short of excuses. What was I scared of? I wasn't afraid of work or getting up at 5.30 a.m. or making a pot load of money. I wouldn't miss the new house at home, because it wasn't a patch on the old house. I wouldn't miss the parish dances in the hall or the funerals that we'd need to go to or the long Masses on Sundays and the endless holy days. The men's side and the women's side. The slow set and the feel of corsets and under-garments that had no role to play in modern romance. NO! I wanted the bare flesh of New York. The gyrating hips of a city that doesn't sleep. Buckets of French fries instead of buckets of water from the well. I needed somewhere to sin out loud. To look up at the tall build-ings and shout, 'Who gives a shite how the windows get washed?' All my life I was peddling like billy-o to stay still – time to freewheel for a while.

I told Kevin I was going to stay. He didn't break down or anything. He said, 'Right ... How long, or do ya know?' I didn't know. By the time we got back to our uncle's house, I was nearly a New Yorker. Almost had an accent. Began to drop the long-step culchie walk from home. I wasn't on cloud nine, but I was up near seven.

The uncle had a few questions to bring me back down to earth. Where was I going to live? Was I going to work without a work visa? What about my parents? What about my work at home? I had no answers. Luckily, he had some. I would live with him till I got sorted ...

work for cash for as long as possible and ring home to say goodbye.

Right ...

I was staying in America – in New York. All the positives were there. Alongside the negatives. The best thing to do was not to think about anything too much ... and I didn't. Naivety had its virtues.

The best place to source work was in a bar. Uncle Michael had a bar in Woodlawn – the Shamrock. Bottles of Budweiser and Miller Lite. No Guinness. American bars were different to the bars in Carrigallen. The Irish pub was a place for friends to meet; the American bar was a place for strangers to meet. I wasn't looking for friends. Anyway, you can't make friends in a bar – friendships formed in bars are friendships built on sand. The jukebox in the Shamrock was everyone's friend with 'Dirty Old Town' on repeat. The Pogues' new version of the song rang out as an Irish anthem. The fact that it was about an English town didn't cost us a thought. We were claiming it as we claimed the Pogues, wallowing in misfortune and despair. We have always been the unwanted underdog. And in 1985 New York, it was me against the rest – me and 'Dirty Old Town'.

'You're a full back, I'd say ... or centre back?' an anonymous mound of Irishness blurted from a barstool.

I had noticed him looking at me. Anonymous mounds of Irishmen were everywhere in the Shamrock Bar. He continued, 'Naw, not mobile enough for centre back. Full back, I'd say. Or midfield. Or we could stick you in full forward, if we were down a couple of points in the last few minutes.'

I wasn't sure if I was supposed to respond.

'Or maybe you don't play at all?'

'Oh, I do,' I said. 'And you're right – full back and midfield. And full forward ... the odd time.'

I went over to shake his hand.

'Where the fuck are ya going with the hand out?' That put me back a bit. 'Where are ya from?'

'Leitrim.'

'I met a fella from Leitrim once. Was he your brother?'

'I wouldn't say so.'

'Is there anyone else in Leitrim apart from you and your brother?'

'A few ...'

'A sense of humour anyways ...'

This man had no sense of humour. In fact, he couldn't be more bitter. Bitter about home, bitter about America. Bitter about the past, the present and 'that fucking song on that bastard of a jukebox in the corner there'. His name was 'Shovels' McGrath. Michael

McGrath, someone said he was, but he was only ever called Shovels. I'd have known why if he had let me shake his hand. But he was as cantankerous as he was cagey – an arrowed stare from a worn-out face. You'd know when Shovels was looking at you … he'd put a hole in a wall with a look.

'You're not long here. I'd know by your trousers …' Shovels was right again. 'Have you work?'

Now he really had my attention. 'No, not yet,' I said. 'I've only just decided to stay.'

'Come down to 52nd Street and Third tomorrow morning. You'll see a construction elevator with a Galway flag sticking out of it. Get on it and go up to the 114th floor and shout, "STOP YA BASTARD," and the wee Puerto Rican will let you out and tell ya to have a nice day. But don't pay any heed to him because he's full of shite. Just ask for Shovels McGrath.'

And that was it! I had a job, a start. And Shovels McGrath went back to dissecting bystanders with his glare.

I didn't know what the job was, and he didn't know what jobs I could do – that was strange. I didn't know what to wear and even if I did, all I had was jeans and runners. My uncle asked some fairly obvious questions too. What was the company's name? What were the wages? Who or what was Shovels McGrath? Was I not still on vacation? I had no answers. Yes, I was still on vacation, but maybe a few days' work would give me a quick taste of the place and help me make up my mind once and for all.

The next morning, I got up at 4 a.m. I knew my sense of direction wasn't great, so I was allowing time for getting lost. I walked from Liebig Avenue in Riverdale to 261st and Broadway ... Got an Express Bus downtown, down through Harlem, past Central Park – all the places I knew so well from cop shows on television. I arrived at my destination far too early. What was I going to do now? The smell of street food and fresh coffee everywhere – everyone eating on the go.

The word 'delicatessen' was new to me. At the time in Ireland, we'd go to Dublin and back without stopping for tea or coffee or chicken fillet rolls the size of a small farm. There was no takeaway tea or coffee in Ireland. Or takeaway anything – everything was left where it was. You ate a good feed before you left the house, went to the toilet and didn't eat or drink or stop for a pee till you arrived back home – bursting to go, and hungry and relatively thin. There was nothing relatively thin about the ones in New York. They were all hanging out of rolls and hotdogs and breakfast in a bucket. Not a good place for a lad who loved to eat.

I eventually got a coffee. Even though 'ordinary' coffee didn't seem to be that popular. No matter how loud or slow I said it.

'How can I help you, sir?'

'Just an ordinary coffee, please.'

'What kind of coffee?'

'OR ... DAN ... RE.'

I said it loads of times and that slow ... but no.

Eventually: 'We've got regular coffee ...?'

'That's it. Regular coffee.'

I was exhausted by the time I got hoisted up to the 114th floor. The 114th floor was empty – no walls, no ceilings, no nothing, just a stack of plasterboard – or 'Sheetrock', as they called it – and that was it. No one there except Shovels McGrath. Shovels sat on the Sheetrock reading the paper, drinking his tea and devouring a bacon bagel.

'You're early. I don't know if that's a good sign or a bad sign.' He didn't look like a man that was going to tear into work. He said, 'We were supposed to be starting this job here today, but unless you have a pocket full of skyhooks that we can hang this Sheetrock on, we're fucked! Talk to yourself there till I finish me breakfast.'

The passenger door

'Seamus ... Seamus, wake up! Shouldn't you be at work?'
I didn't know where I was. My cousin Maureen shaking
me and laughing her head off. 'How do you like New
York ... huh?' It was 8.30 a.m. Work started at 8 a.m. in
Manhattan. I was never late for work! I was now.

'Seamus, you're late for work!'

My head was in a tangle. I'll be sacked, or was I
sacked? What happened yesterday? Think ... Did I
go to the bar and get rat-arsed ...? No, but why can't
I remember? I'm so tired ... and emotional. I feel like
crying ... but I can't cry ... not in front of my cousin.

My cousin Maureen was sixteen at the time. Going
about in big fluffy slippers and laughing at her Irish
cousin who couldn't think straight. Why was my brain
not working? The house was so quiet. Maybe it was
only 4.30? I checked my watch. No – 8.35.

'And you didn't even say goodbye to your brother ...'
Kevin had gone home, the lads had gone back and I

wasn't with them. I had stayed in New York to make my fortune and me still in bed at 8.30 a.m.

Wait a minute ... The footballers were flying home on Saturday ... yesterday ... so ... today is ... Sunday!

'I'm not supposed to be at work ... today is Sunday ...'

Maureen was now falling around the place. I should have been so annoyed, but I was just relieved. I hadn't missed work. I was two days into my new job and I hadn't been sacked. I spotted my runners by the boiler. I was sleeping in the basement with the boiler and the big American washing machine – that looked familiar. My runners were covered in concrete.

'Mum isn't very subtle, cousin. In case you didn't know ... she'll kill you if you wear those sneakers into this house again.'

And then Maureen left. 'Enjoy your day off, cousin ...' She skipped up the concrete steps, then turned back. 'Oh, just to let you know. If you're still here when my dad gets back, he's taking you to Mass. So you might want to go for a walk or something.' And then she was finally gone.

And then I began to remember ...

I watched Shovels McGrath eat his breakfast that first morning – I should have known then what I was in for. You can tell a lot about the way a man eats. I had seen that for myself. Seen the men coming in for the dinner after helping with the hay or silage. Seen the short grip on the knife and fork; the thumb being used as a balance as they horsed big mouthfuls of spuds and cabbage into their snarling mouths. You can tell the barometers of control a man has when you watch him eat. Most men I knew didn't have any control. Except my father. Because, apart from the soft mouth and the constant blowing of the soup and the tea, he caressed his food. Like he did his work ... Like he did his life.

Shovels shovelled his food and gulped the tea. 'These fucking Yanks can't make tea. That's dishwater, that. There's a place out on Long Island and they make the tea in an iron teapot. Jayus, it's great tea. I do often go to it of a Sunday just for the tea.'

'Are you living out there?' I thought that was a fair enough question.

'What the fuck would I be living out there for? Sure that's miles away from anywhere.'

'Oh ...'

'Don't I live up your way – Woodlawn. I'm shacked up with a Black woman up there this years. Don't know what she does be saying half the time, but she's fair warm in herself. Some body on her. Jayus, that's what ya want says you. Take your points and the goals will come. Come on! This joint won't be ready till tomorrow.'

Shovels squinched his paper cup and bagel wrap into a miniature ball, and with the motion of a natural footballer, he kicked it against one of the many dusty windows that surrounded the 114th floor. I don't know why, but I found solace in that.

'Can you drive, Leitrim?' Fellas like Shovels never gave anyone the respect of calling them by their right name – from now on, I was called 'Leitrim'. I could have been called worse.

'I can,' I said, anxious to answer in the positive at every opportunity! He put his hand in his pocket and took out a set of keys and tossed them in the air as someone would toss a football. I rose like Jack O'Shea and caught them. Then I started thinking: *Is he really going to make me drive in New York ... in this traffic ... on the wrong side ... HELP!* I decided to say nothing.

We descended the construction elevator, the Puerto Rican attendant trying desperately to brighten our day. 'Weeeee're at the bottom, my friends. May the sun always be inside of you,' he said, putting a twist on the old Irish prayer. But the sun was not inside me or Shovels. All I could see was major pile-ups in downtown Manhattan. Surely he wasn't expecting me to drive?

We walked a half block to a brown Transit. 'Click that button,' he said. I did. The hazards of the van flashed and I saw my chance. I quickly threw the keys as high up into the air as I could and ran round the passenger side and jumped in. I then realised I was not in the passenger seat, but the driver's seat. The other door opened, and Shovels got in. And he was right thick now. He handed me the keys and said, 'Don't ever throw keys about like that again. You're not in Leitrim now.' Then, 'Have ya no work boots? Or what kind of an omadhaun comes to work in a pair of soft shoes? Start her up there and go where I tell you.'

Driving a van in Manhattan, while taking instructions from a thick Connemara alcoholic, is like trying to land a jumbo jet in a blizzard. I don't know what it's like to land a jumbo jet, but if it's anything like driving that van in Manhattan, then I wouldn't recommend it. I was pale with hopelessness. Stopped breathing on 53rd Street and didn't start up again until we were on the New Jersey Turnpike – my life flashing before me. Or was that it in my rear-view mirror? He'd tell me that there was a turn coming up, and when I'd look over for confirmation, he'd be pretending to be asleep or dead. I wanted him to be dead. I have never hated anyone so much.

'Pull in here, Leitrim.' I pulled in and my hands were stuck to the steering wheel – I couldn't let go. I was closer to tears than I had ever been in my life. This was some kind of test. I was unaware of bullying or coercive behaviour at the time. I thought that times like this were simply a test. That life was a continuous stream of uncomfortable moments that would eventually pass – making way for the next slice of persecution. I didn't know enough to say, 'Stick your keys and your job up the Hudson River!' I was never that strong.

'Ya did all right, Leitrim …' As if that was going to repair the psychological damage caused. It didn't … but it helped. I was able to extract myself from the van. What next?

'This is a prick of a job,' Shovels explained. 'There's concrete arriving here in a few minutes and it can only be dumped there in the lobby. There's buckets in the back of the van to bring it down into the basement. I have help comin' so you won't be on your own. Portlaoise is down there now; you can give him a hand to screed it, when you're doing nothing. Don't stand in the one spot too long in them shoes or your feet will start to fall off. The concrete is a hoor.'

Shovels opened the back of the van and fired out six or seven plastic buckets, got into the driver's seat and drove off. What kind of outfit was this?

Portlaoise came up to see where was the help. As frightened-looking as me, but a bit older. Marcus

Lawler, his right name was. He was sucking hard on a fag – that wasn't a good sign. Same unprepared look as me. 'I was working in a chicken factory. I know nothing about concrete.' He then looked at the fag in his hand. He was after taking three consecutive pulls. 'Ah now, shite. Look at this now. I didn't smoke till a week ago … Where am I going with the fag?'

He threw the cigarette on the ground and jumped on it – just like I had wanted to jump on Shovels McGrath.

'Do you know this Shovels McGrath?' he said.

'No,' was all I had time to say and then then the concrete truck arrived … followed by another and another. There was no time to question our sanity – only get to work.

I laid concrete with my father over the years. No trucks … no big pour … just me and him and my brother heading off to Killerrin with a transport box full of gravel and a couple of shovels and two bags of cement. A five-to-one mix and we'd patch up some part of the yard; my father as particular as if we were patching a runway. Days like those on the outlying farm were never my cup of tea … but compared to what was about to take place, they were heaven.

Myself and Marcus Lawler and a wee auld fella from Tyrone bucketed three truckloads of concrete down two flights of stairs ... cursed it and screeded it ... even brought some of it back up the stairs, and it only took us ten hours. I was a fit man at the time, and yes, I was tired – I had done most of the bucketing – but Marcus and Tyrone were completely jacked. It was like trying to stand two old mattresses against the wall, as I got them ready for their lift. Shovels came back at 8 p.m. and surveyed the work without letting slip any element of surprise at how the hell we'd managed it. I got in the back of the van for the journey home – the darkness and emptiness a luxury.

'Fifty-second and Third in the morning, Leitrim!' Shovels roared as I emerged from the back of the van. And, against none of my principles – because I didn't have any – I said I'd see him there.

Big money

So, it was simply tiredness that had caused my confusion ... I was delighted it had provided my cousin Maureen with such entertainment. I had often been tired before from a hard day at the hay or in the bog. Or a championship game in the height of summer when you'd strain every sinew in an attempt to bring victory back to your parish or your county. But this was way beyond that ... I was completely flummoxed. Then I heard a voice. 'How ya doing there, buddy?' My uncle came down into the basement dressed like he was getting his Confirmation – the shine off him! He had been for a cycle and a run and had two hundred sit-ups under his belt. He was forty years my senior. 'So how was working with Mike McGrath ...' Uncle Michael had dug up some information on one of his mysterious customers. And he had his suspicions. 'He claims he played for Galway in Croke Park, but man, I think he's a bum. Did he pay you?'

My wages? Yes, he did pay me – I think. I remembered he gave me an envelope and said something smart like, 'You're in the money now, Leitrim.' Had I opened it? How much was it? I didn't want to check in front of my uncle.

'Yeah, got paid … big enough money …' I said.

'I thought you'd be ready for Mass. Did Maureen not tell you? You have six minutes. I haven't been late for Mass in St Margaret's in over twenty-seven years.' And he left.

Mass! That's all I needed! I grabbed my – now – work trousers and searched through the pockets for my wages. An unopened envelope. I must have been saving the surprise for morning. It felt like a good wad – two days' work would be at least $300 dollars. I opened it up. There was a $100 bill on top. Maybe it's a thousand – American money is all the same size, be it a hundred, a fifty, a ten or a one. There was $167 in my wage packet. Yes, a $100 bill on top, but the rest was mostly ones and fives. The bastard Shovels McGrath! And what I'd gone through for this! I couldn't remember the second day, but on the basis of my memories from the first, this was a complete nonsense.

I got dressed as quickly and as fancy as I could. Uncle Michael was waiting in the porch counting down the seconds. 'You only just made it, buddy.'

We stepped out into Sunday morning. It's hard not to fall in love with New York in the fall. The trees lining our short walk to St Margaret's Church on Riverdale Avenue were picture perfect. A glorious day, we'd call it at home – here, it was just another day.

The Americans don't get stuck into Mass the same way as we do; they didn't seem to have the same amount of shame or guilt – or the same amount of hay down. They looked like they could sit there all day and admire their religion. Religion is supposed to wear you down, drag you from one desperate stage of your life to the next. Religion had slipped over most of these ones – all straight-backed as they walked up for Communion. Could they not feel the weight? The basket came round – of course it did. Mass without a collection would be like a parish concert without a raffle. I would normally throw in a few coins, but it was all paper money here. A dollar would do, especially with the money I was on. I rooted through my wage packet for a dollar, being reminded once again of my first two days' wages. I threw the green note into the basket, only to suddenly realise that it was not a dollar, but a hundred dollars! The $100 sign was waving at me across the edge of the basket and there was only a millisecond where I could have rectified my mistake without making a scene.

I missed it. Would I go after the little Black man who had politely placed the basket in front of me? Not in a million years. I looked to my uncle for guidance, but he had his eyes closed in prayer. What was he praying for now? Two of the hardest days' work in my life – two days of applied slavery – and now, nearly two-thirds of my wages gone floating away. The only one on big money in this country was St Margaret's Church on Riverdale Avenue. If there were ever any doubts over my stupidity, this was clarification. The stupidest, tiredest, unluckiest human being alive!

And speaking of tired, my uncle was now asleep beside me. That somehow gave me comfort. So, he wasn't the Duracell Bunny after all. Yes, he got up in the middle of the night and ran and cycled and sat up till the cows came home – but he also slept eight hours a day in five-minute segments. It's important to know that your parents or family are not superheroes or Duracell bunnies. Michael was one of those competitive overlords – had to be the first up and the first out; had to hold the record for time-keeping and dieting and eating broccoli; had the straightest hedge and shortest grass in the Bronx – a fully Americanised Irishman who dreamed of home in Leitrim till the day he died in 2022 at the tender age of ninety-seven.

Suddenly, I had a flashback. Right there in the chapel – in the church of St Margaret, with my uncle snoring and the loss of my $100 still smarting – I remembered. I had made peace yesterday with Shovels. Yes, I turned up for work on Saturday morning. I was on the 114th floor of 52nd and Third. I was early, but there were loads of people there with tools and more Sheetrock and aluminium studding and 'fire in the hole' – all sorts of banging and shouting and yahooing. Welcome to the world of construction in downtown New York.

'You're early, Leitrim, but that's good. Mustn't have worked you hard enough yesterday. Today's another day. Most of these guys got here at five – want to get away for their Saturday golf. I can't stand that golf, but they're doing me a favour. You know how to cut Sheetrock?' I looked around and saw a lad cutting a sheet with a Stanley knife.

'Yeah, I think so,' I said.

'You're some chancer, Leitrim. You'll fit in well around here. Finish your coffee and I'll be back for you in ten minutes.'

Shovels went off. He seemed energised. I didn't know if that was a good thing or not.

I had a good study of what was going on around me. At first glance, it looked hectic and complicated, but it was really straightforward. An entire floor being set out into offices and corridors with an aluminium track Hilti-ed to the floor and one to the ceiling – stud, cut to length and placed in the track. *Zip-zip* went the screw guns. No screw guns in Tommy Reilly's. We had only got as far as the Yankee screwdriver in 1985. New York was leading the way in construction and a type of carpentry that didn't seem to contain any wood products. This suited the Irish carpenters, most of whom weren't really carpenters in the first place. It was simple enough ... I thought.

Shovels returned with another mood. Not a very endearing mood. A caustic approach that would last the day. He summoned me to grab a toolbelt and tools and follow him. And so, the game began. The game being to guess what Shovels wanted or was thinking. Not an easy game, as he could change the rules at any time.

'I suppose you're a metric man,' was his first accusation.

'I can do both,' I replied.

Metric measurements were what youngsters were growing up with in Ireland – a nod to Europe and the EEC. I grew up with metric too, but I also was well accustomed to feet and inches from working with my father and Tommy Reilly and the couple of summers spent in the Engineering in Newtown. Good job, because there were no metric measurements on this tape.

I realised after a short time working with Shovels that he was a narcissistic conglomeration of hurt. He took the most contrary corner of the 114th floor and proceeded to shout and roar incoherent instructions. He would kick, knock, reef inanimate objects out of his way to get snarling face to face with me. To stare me one of his stares. To push me to the edge or to a place where I would crumble. But I wasn't having it. If he had put me up on a wall plate a hundred storeys high or plunged me into even a small pool of water, I'd have begged for mercy. But this? This was just Lego. And although we only ever had two or three Lego bricks at a time growing up, I knew how it worked, and Shovels McGrath wasn't getting the better of me.

If the day before was a physical marathon, this was another – with the mind games of a psychopath thrown in.

'Eighty-one up … fourteen in … soft corner … seven … twenty and a half … sloping back to naught.'

To the untrained ear, that's just gobbledygook. And it could have been to me too. Only, I could see what Shovels was looking at. And I cut to order. And 99 per cent of the time it was perfect. He even swapped roles with me, trying to catch me out. I called the measurements and he cut – it was still right. He made me climb, crawl, crawl backways; made me balance sheets on my head and hold them in one hand. And I used every brain cell and sinew to keep up and stay up and get back up and between silent prayers and inward cursing – and a rummage through my back catalogue of thick wit. I not only kept going – I excelled. Until Shovels let out a groan …

'Enough, Leitrim … enough done for the day. I'm sick of ya, ya big bollix ya!'

And that was it. The ordeal was over.

He handed me an envelope and said, 'That's for yesterday. You'll get paid for today along with next week's wages. If you come back next week. I wouldn't blame ya if ya didn't. But you're a good one, Leitrim. What did you do at home?' I said I was a carpenter. 'And why didn't ya tell me that in the first place, ya dipstick? I have some lovely handy jobs for you next week.'

Frank

I was waiting for a phone to become available on Bainbridge Avenue. It was a cold and dry evening in the Bronx. It was Monday, the 6th of January 1986. Available phones on Bainbridge Avenue were like hens' teeth at the weekend. Not so much this evening ... no queue ... I just had to wait a few more minutes till someone here or in Ireland hung up. Bainbridge was a hotbed of phone crime at the time. Some young Irish waitress would scribble the credit card number of a customer on a piece of paper and that same number would be distributed among the Irish and used for phone calls to home. Every public phone on Bainbridge – and there were quite a few – was red hot from over and back idle conversation trying to get the most out of the illegal manoeuvre. If we were paying for the call, it would be short and to the point: 'Send teabags – send sausages – Send Tayto. Oh, and how's Granny?' But because it was free, it was: 'So, any other news? How's the calf that was sick? How is Daddy's knee? Did yer man come out to fix the immersion?' And from the Irish side: 'What time is it there? What's your weather like? Are ya going to Mass?' An Olympic event of petty Irish small talk, under the umbrella of phoning home.

I rang on Christmas Day, from my uncle's house. Short and sweet and devoid of any sentiment.

'Everything is great. Happy Christmas. Do you want to talk to Michael?'

Christmas Day was my only day off. Back to work the following day. That suited me. The less time off the better. Nothing to do on a day off. No Mullen market or driving about dreaming. Or putting in stereos or buying tapes. Here it was just me and my new roommate, Brian. Brian was my first cousin ... a couple of years younger than me. Brian had Down's syndrome and was my new best friend. He was everyone's best friend – enough love and joy to go round the whole house. Yes, he had his moments, but compared to the rest of us, he was an angel and an inspiration, and I cherish the time I shared with him. We were the lads: me and him. Always out-numbered and outmanoeuvred by his sisters, Maureen, Eileen and Maggie. And although they were aged from seventeen down to eleven, they were full of the female deviousness which must be secretly passed on through dolls and make-up. Me and Brian never had a chance.

My uncle's house was a house of war – and warmth and devilment. I was lucky to get the chance to share it, but it wasn't home, and it wasn't permanent. 'I'll get out of your way soon,' I kept saying to Michael, hoping there was no panic. And there wasn't. But in truth, I wasn't sure about my bright future in America. I loved New York; loved the thought of it … the feel of it … but I wasn't really in New York. I was in a purgatory between here and there, and there and here. Smack bang in a no man's land. But Ireland and Irishness remained my currency, and nothing at the time was making me rich.

For the while I was there, I had only once found the real New York. I had arranged to meet a friend of someone from home in downtown Manhattan. We met in a bar, but not an Irish bar. I hopped on the 1 train at 242nd Street and got off in Times Square. Took in the sights and the sounds and the smells – and the energy. And, boy, did New York have energy! Walked into a trendy bar on 39th Street. No 'Dirty Old Town' on the jukebox, no tears on the floor … and no preamble with my friend of a friend on how everyone was doing at home. Just me and him surrounded by TVs and sport and America. The New York Yankees – the Knicks – the Giants – the Rangers. We talked about basketball and ice

hockey and places to eat, and didn't compare anything
to home or never mentioned the wet year in Ireland. For
those few hours, I was living in America. The rest of the
time, I felt like I was tethered to a leprechaun ... carrying clods of turf around in me underpants to protect me
from Americans and AIDS and adulthood.

I grabbed the next available phone on Bainbridge
Avenue, still warm from 'Miss you's and the 'Bye-bye-
bye's. I rang the old familiar number of home. Almost
immediately: 'Hello there. We were wondering would ya
ring. What time is it with you? How is Michael's back?
What's your weather like? The weather's a sight here ...'

I listened to familiar tones of unfamiliar politeness,
probing for, but not inviting, any talk of trouble or
glitches in my distanced existence. Most problems over-
seas were covered by prayers and constant worrying.
Phone calls were merely for reassurance. Irish parenting
in the '80s was hands-off and complicated.

I felt better after the phone call – good to have it out
of the way. There was no news from home, apart from
the death notices and the shocking news that Christmas
was still in full swing in Carrigallen. The last of the
dances and dinner dances were still taking place and the
turkey soup was still lovely after a week without being
in the fridge. And Pat Fitch had a new car ordered for

January – always a major talking point. And the tractors had to be drained at night due to the frost. If there
had been any more news, I'd have had to lie down for
an hour.

More pressing for me was that I was still on relatively small money in New York – and that I didn't
have a social security number, because I was an 'illegal
alien'. I had never been an illegal anything, let alone an
alien. But not to fear. My uncle and the wider churchgo-
ing Irish community had come up with a social security
number and a change of name. From now on I was
to be known as Frank – Frank Blessing. A blessing –
a miracle – a born-again American! And I had a new
job, working as a carpenter for Sal Developments with
a pending acceptance into the local Carpenters' Union.
Twenty dollars an hour in 1986 was not to be sneezed at
or ignored, but the born-again American was ignoring
the calls of 'Hey Frank!', 'What ya think, Frank?', 'Can
you hear me, Frank?' and 'Why doesn't Frank answer?'
Frank was taking some time to get used to being called
Frank. I must have come across as being very ignorant
or very deaf or both. I didn't mind being called Leitrim –
but Frank? I wasn't a Frank. The Franks I knew were
older and wiser. They carried cloth hankies to blow
their noses – I was still wiping my nose in my sleeve.

I would never be a proper Frank. I wasn't mature enough or willing to be mature enough. The one thing I hated was maturity and sensibility. Being silly or the ability to be silly is most underrated. There's enough long-faced Franks in the world. I was never comfortable with adding to that.

On the 11th of March 1986, myself and Donie McLoughlin walked down 261st Street towards Broadway. Donie said, 'Am I right, or is it your birthday?

'You're right. Twenty-one.'

'Happy birthday.'

'Thanks.'

We were now on Broadway. I always say I celebrated my twenty-first birthday on Broadway. On 261st Street. A long way from 42nd Street – but I was still on Broadway.

Donie was a rock of sense – always lived in the moment. A chameleon, he adapted and fitted in wherever he went. I didn't. I didn't have his powers. I always played along ... always talked the talk. But that evening – the evening of my twenty-first – as we sang, 'My feet are here on Broadway ...' I was as mixed up as a postman in the Sahara Desert. My feet might have been on Broadway, but my heart wasn't. I was thinking of going home. I didn't know why I was leaving the land of milk and honey and I didn't know why I was going home, but I was. And before I did, I had a few things to do.

I was now getting my hands on the big bucks. I was now in the Carpenters' Union which paid $20 an hour – $40 an hour for overtime. With a bit of luck, I might have enough money to pay for my flight and the skiing trip to Vermont and the weekend in Washington DC to visit my aunts. I also needed to get fit. I was going home to play football. I needed to be able to run. I had forgotten how to run because I had discovered the gym.

The gym – what a great idea for a young sportsman. I had never been to a gym in Ireland. Winter training in Ireland included running with your head down around a dimly lit field in Drumshanbo with the wind, sleet and rain beating the head off ya like an exasperated English teacher. The thought of a hundred sit-ups in the mud – not good. But what was the alternative? Gyms were too controlled for Irishmen. And when I went to one of them for the first time, I declined all help and direction. I just stuck the pin in the bottom hole and nearly put out me egg-bag liftin' and puffin' and gruntin'. But I lifted every pound of weight in that gym. Black lads standing round me wondering who was the bright orange motherfucker pumping all that iron. I had to call on every ounce of ignorance to do ten repetitions on every piece of machinery in that there gym. 'Who de man?,' they shouted as I lay poleaxed on the floor after an hour's workout. Within seven weeks, I was as big as a house and as stiff as a board and unable to run. Now, I was going to have to undo all that, so I could get on the plane. And the other thing – I was going to have to stop eating. I had got into the habit of zigzagging across Times Square – going from McDonald's to Burger King and back. The restaurants were at war with each other at the time. I can only say, I supported both.

The last hurrah

'Where is Ben? Have you seen Ben?'

Ben was nowhere to be seen. He was last seen on a snowy Mount Ellen – pissed. It was very inconsiderate of him to get lost or killed while another member of our skiing party was about to score. I wasn't often a scorer, but a certain 'Jenny' was playing ball and I was lining up a free kick. It wasn't going to be a defining moment in our lives as we were both well cut, but a score is a score, and as Shovels McGrath would say, 'Take your points and the goals will come.'

There is no romance between these pages because I was useless at romance – never got the right run at it. There was always a missing ingredient – like the girl. Or the name of the girl. I had conspired to miss out on endless romances by my lack of attention to detail. Like when I went out with a girl called … Well, that was the thing, I didn't know her name. I met her at a dance in the Mayflower Ballroom in Drumshanbo when I was nineteen. We hit it off. I had asked her her name and she had told me, but I had forgotten it. Something like Hilda or Hilary. But it wasn't either of those names because they're English names and this girl had an Irish-sounding name beginning with Hill or Hilly. It just wouldn't come to me. And the thing is, when you start going out with a girl, it's important to know her name. And the longer you leave it – especially if she told you and you forgot it – the stranger it seems to not know it. Women can be funny like that. And the annoying thing was, when we met her friends, she'd introduce them: 'This is Michelle,' or 'Catriona'. Then she'd introduce me to them: 'This is Seamus.' But she never mentioned her own name and I couldn't find out what it was. And I couldn't start guessing. I couldn't call her something she wasn't, and I couldn't ask her friends because that seemed strange too. After about five weeks of not knowing her name and avoiding all contact with my friends in case they'd ask, 'Who is this?', it's not as if I could say, 'Oh it's just my girl-friend. I don't know what she's called, but I'll look for a tag later on. Maybe her mother sewed her name into her knickers.'

On the sixth week, myself and Martina split up. That was her name – not Hill or Hilly … Martina. She was lovely and was very fond of me ... but I couldn't let it go any further. I broke it off.

I said, 'Look, whatever your name is ...'

Of course, I didn't say that at all. I said, 'Listen honey, this isn't really working.'

She was distraught – broke down in tears at the mineral bar in the hall in Ballinamore. And I felt so sorry for her, this could have been avoided if she had said her name louder and more clearly in the beginning ... and maybe with a little wink, like my mother used to do when she was passing on important information. But there was no going back now, it was done.

Immediately after I broke it off, three different people came over and said:

'Are you okay, Martina?'

'Oh, Martina.'

'Poor Martina!'

Poor me! Why didn't someone tell me? I had heard people calling her Martina before, but I had thought they were getting her mixed up with someone else, because she was Hill or Hilly (*no she wasn't ya bollix!*). I then called her Martina seventeen times in a row ... but it was too late. I had messed up the whole thing, again.

Some fellas seemed to thrive in the presence of women; fellas who were thick as turnips and couldn't kick snow off a rope. What did they talk about? I was never any good at the small talk. What do you say to a woman you fancy – apart from, 'Please fill out this form, stating your full name and address'? I was useless. But Jenny was different. She was one of our skiing party in Vermont. Donie McLoughlin and myself and a few of his friends – because I didn't have any – had spent the weekend in Vermont skiing. Well, the skiing was available, and we had all tried it on the baby slopes. But Irish people skiing doesn't work. Irish people going on holiday is one thing, but don't put them on the side of a slippy mountain with anything other than good tyres.

That's where I bumped into Jenny – during one of our many pile-ups at the bottom of Mount Ellen. She had been with our group, and I hadn't really noticed her, but whatever happened when we slithered into each other at the bottom of the hill, it caused a spark and a sudden urge to go to the bar and drink Miller and Bud and keep saying, 'That was so funny.' She had asked me several times what my cabin was like, but I didn't take the hint – thought she might have been into interior decorating or just a cabin enthusiast. She eventually said, 'Well do you want the ride or not?' I wasn't fully sure what she meant. It had never been put so bluntly to me before. What about the romance, the cheek-to-cheek reversing and manoeuvring?

Was that not going to be part of it? Were we just going to go at it like Tosh Rourke's bull and one of our lookin' heifers? Maybe I was overthinking it? Maybe I should just do what nature was telling me. Nature was only telling me one thing. Nature was ready ... but was I?

Me and Jenny were all agog with nature and rubbin' against each other. We made our way to a cabin – not my cabin ... more like a stick shed. I was about to burst with nature, when I heard the cry 'Where's Ben? We can't find Ben!' Me with what felt like Big Ben in my trousers, just about to strike midnight! Jenny, all flushed and beautiful, said, 'We better help find him.' And that was it. The nearest I got. I could see God smiling. *Well done, my child.* It was probably God who had sent Ben up the mountain – the biggest dose of a gobshite from Clare – on the summit of Mount Ellen, where he let himself off down the slope, backways with a fag in his mouth. He smashed into the first tree in his path and collapsed. Half concussed – half asleep – fully drunk. He was lucky, they said. We weren't. He was returned to our party on a snowmobile. A warning to all. Life is short – live it while you can! I was doing everything in my power not to.

I got a letter from home. Not my mother's handwriting, but my dad's. What in the honour of all that was sacred did he want?

Dear Seamus ... That sounded strange.

I hope you are still getting on all right in
New York.

I hope your weather is better than here.
We're supposed to get another wet year. But
we'll have to make do with what we get.

Your car is still going well. It's a great car.
I got Pat McGee to do a few jobs on it, so
it'll be going well when you get back.

Me and your mother will meet you in
Shannon.

You won't find that now.
Bye for now.
Daddy

I put Johnny McEvoy's 20 *Greatest Hits* into my
Walkman, listened again and found solace along 'The
Old Bog Road'.

My father wasn't a poet, but sometimes he could
soften words like a poet. Nothing in his letter was
romantic – rain and the car and Pat McGee. Nothing
romantic about Pat McGee. But I was full sure I was
doing the right thing by going home. I'd make a terrible millionaire, a terrible Yank. After two televisions,
what else would I buy? I'd be forty stone if I stayed

in America; no gym would have enough weights to keep me pumping. No. I would take my rather large and muscular arse back to the Emerald Isle and forage further into the dark depths of despair. You never know what you might find in the dark.

My uncle Michael was disappointed. He felt he had let me down. That America had let me down – but it hadn't. I loved America. I loved New York. And my uncle Michael couldn't have done any more for me. He was a most wonderful and peculiar man. Full of spirit and enthusiasm. He would have loved a son who played sport like I did, but I wasn't his son. He had a very special son – Brian! And my uncle Michael showered love on that boy like no other. And apart from a weakness for *The Benny Hill Show* on repeat, my cousin Brian was perfect. He had a way of teaching people about themselves. But I still wasn't sure who I was. All I knew was that I wasn't Frank Blessing – although I did get Frank into the Carpenters' Union. His final wage was $1,195. And that's the wage I would quote when anyone asked me 'Was the money as good as they say?'

'Oh yes it was.'

I said goodbye to Aunt Margaret. I could see the relief on her face. Not glad to get rid of me – just glad she didn't have to feed me anymore. I had been a constant challenge to her saucepan rack. I said goodbye to my cousins, the girls – cheeky as bedamned. Brian gave me a hug and a tap on the head as if I was one of Benny Hill's sidekicks. And that was it. Mike, as he was called over there, dropped me back to where he found me. JFK airport. The tightest of handshakes and I was away. Goodbye, USA!

Never one to look back, I began to think of home and the rain and what Pat McGee and the Auld Lad had done with my car. Of course, it was raining at Shannon. Of course, the Auld Pair underwhelmed me with their welcome, but I was back, and once again, very much, at large.

The returned Yank

No matter where in the world you've been, you will always be struck by the green coming in to land at Dublin or Shannon airports – or any Irish airport. We do green well. But this was a wicked March morning. There was some green, but there was also lots of dull brown and grey. I was home. Airports are not nice places. Shannon was no worse than any other. I collected my suitcases and emerged from the womb of the arrival tunnel. My rural farmer parents trying desperately to hide their rural farmer look. The Auld Lad's cap gave it away. Mammy, who couldn't stand public gaze, hid behind him – his long legs that became his body without any waist. 'Hello there,' I said. The 'there' added to give the greeting more warmth.

'Hello there, you,' was the warmth of their reply. Mammy moved in for a three-quarter hug – an action not often attempted in our family. An action as unnatural as it was clumsy, but it mimicked what was going on around us and somehow helped us to blend in.

'Was there many on the plane?' my father asked.

'Aye, it was nearly full,' I said, giving far too much weight to an out-of-context question.

'Have you a cold?' my mother asked.

I hadn't. Unconsciously I was talking in a deeper voice than the one I had left with. I had adjusted my voice and accent to a New York setting while I was away, so that they might understand me better and accept me – just to make life easier for everyone. But I was so aware of the horror caused by ones coming home from America and England with an accent that I had overcompensated with my voice reset, and I was now talking like a professor of cow dung with a chest infection.

'We're not parked in a great spot,' Daddy said. Then, 'But there was nowhere else … I don't know if we'll get out.'

And so the idle chat continued. I was home and glad to be home and I didn't need to be met by sophistication or suffocating embraces. I found a part of me at the airport that morning that I didn't know I was missing – the decency and honesty of my parents. I had been in such a hurry to distance myself from them – so afraid of becoming them. But I would never become them. I would never be a patch on my parents.

The road home was long, and although the Auld
Pair had come to get me in my car, I had let my father
drive home. He'd have been disappointed if I didn't let
him show off his skills of navigation and carefulness.
And maybe he was delighted to have me home – the
thought never crossed my mind at the time. Mammy
had brought sandwiches. And whatever outward love
was missing in our public fumblings, it was all there in
the luncheon roll and lettuce sandwiches. Real butter
and salad cream. And onion! How I love onion in a
sandwich. Onion in a sandwich is love. I don't need any
other signs. My mother loved me ... loved all of us ...
and she would never forget the bit of onion.

'Will you be fit to play football tomorrow?' my father
said, looking into the mirror for a reaction. I wasn't fit.
I wasn't injured, but I couldn't run. I had wintered well
in New York. Ate more Quarter Pounders and fries and
apple pies for dessert and pumped iron in the gym. I was
now more akin to the Michelin man than a county man.
What would they think? I was as stiff as a poker. I had
been to Van Cortlandt Park a few days before – togged
out in me Leitrim gear. The togs were as tight as elastic
knickers – the puffed-up thighs of a weight-lifter and
the barrel chest of a wrestler! I attempted to run, but
I had failed at every attempt. Caused a few tremors on

Broadway Avenue. I had arrived in New York as fit and as lean as I had ever been, and now I was like a turkey on steroids. So, NO was the answer to my father's question, but I said, 'Aye, hopefully ... if I don't have jetlag.'

We got back to Drumshangore in late afternoon. I had forgotten that we had built the new bungalow – it had never entered my mind's eye when I thought of home. It still doesn't. My eldest sister Margaret was home for the weekend. Kevin was there, and Geraldine. A family gathering and no remarks passed on my size. Just 'Have you loads of money now?', 'How is Michael?' and 'Guess who died?' I eventually got tired and retired to bed. I was glad to be home, but I wasn't sorry for going away. I was just moving with the flow ... and so it would always be. We weren't a dramatic family. We were steady – always managed to stay afloat – always managed to drift slowly towards the next wave of calamities. And so it was, and so I went to sleep.

The next day was a day of reintroduction. It started with Mass. Outstanding, because I had a new jumper. It wasn't hard to catch the eye in Drumeela. Lots of 'Welcome Home's and 'How long were you away?'s 'Are you going back?' and 'Things are fierce bad in this country ... who'd want to stay here?' And a general feeling of 'You're an awful fool to be coming home.'

My biggest worry was this football match in Cloone at three o'clock. What are they going to think? I could feel my thighs rubbing together as I came down the aisle from Communion. I was bloated. Maybe it was the Communion. Maybe I was retaining water. I needed to do an intense warm-up before the game ... and a really big poo.

Pat Mitchell was his ever-positive self. 'Jakers, you're in some shape, Rourkey ... you'd put us all to shame. I heard you were training like billy-o over there. You'll be some help today.' I wasn't. I was lined out at mid-field. Like, they were giving me space to turn, but it was awful. I couldn't turn. I couldn't run. I needed a head start to get to the centre of the field for the throw-in. Everyone gave me the benefit of the doubt, even the Auld Lad. He said I was never that quick anyway. The new manager of the county team was there. He wasn't as easily deceived. He had been ringing me in America, saying I was crucial to his plans and that I had a big part to play in the Leitrim Senior team and Under-21s. He was one of the reasons I had come home. He rang me that night and told me I needed to lose at least two stone – that I had an arse the size of a small country! I knew he was right, and I remembered that old man in Sligo General Hospital who could judge humans and their athletic limitations by the size of their arses. It was never going to happen for me to lose two stone, but I went with the flow and added salads to my diet and thought really hard about being thin.

I had another problem – I had no job. I couldn't go back to Tommy Reilly after leaving work to go on holiday and then forgetting to return. My parents had rung him to say I was staying in America. But 'it was auld-fashioned enough of me to stay away'. So, it was down to looking in the paper and the small ads. There was a carpenter wanted in Duignan's of Dromod – they made church seating and had thirty or so employed. The money was only middling, and it was 40 minutes away, but it was all there was, and I took it and was glad to get it and that was it. I hated it, but that was beside the point. I had no choice.

At Duignan's I was part of an assembly line putting church seating together – running planks of ash and oak through a four-cutter – joining – gluing – sanding. If people only knew the amount of fucks it took to make a church pew. Handmade, beautifully finished and full of curses from lads who hated sanding and gluing and beautifully finishing. I have never worked in a place where so many people were so disjointed. There was no canteen; everyone sat in their cars and ate their lunch and listened to the radio. Or in my case, ate peanuts and salad and scanned the paper for new diets and a decent job.

In the evenings I trained – dragged my surplus cargo around the perimeters of sports fields in Drumshanbo and Carrick and Carrigallen. A half-hearted attempt to reharness something that had passed. Yes, I was still young, but I no longer had the desire to defy nature and physics and physical proportion. I had known for some time that I was big-boned, that I wasn't a Ferrari. And no matter how much salad I ate, or peanuts, I would never be one. I would always be a Massey Ferguson 135 with double wheels. That broke my heart. And it was nobody's fault, not even mine, and I did try to find things to be grateful for, but there weren't many ... not in my head.

At the weekends, I went to Carrigallen to Harte's hotel – the Kilbrackan Arms – an oasis of colour in my drab world. There was a friendliness about Carrigallen that wasn't unique, but it was special. We didn't really care where you came from or how you got there; not worried about your intentions or your past indiscretions ... only that you stood your round and allowed yourself to be ridiculed as part of our local pastime. You could not get saved in Carrigallen, but you'd have great fun drowning there. We were experts on every aspect of lunacy known to man. Classes were held all day. Newcomers welcome! In the '80s and early '90s, the small town of Carrigallen was awash with twits and halfwits and full-time omadhauns … trainee alcoholics and wasters talking on topics never before discussed. And great singers and ones singing that couldn't sing and arguments over politics and pine martens that no one had ever seen or knew anything about. And lectures from Professor Aidan Harte – English classes that no one understood.

'And how about a recitation?'

'In a little pub in London, Moriarity drank his beer …' or 'I'm livin' in Drumlister …'

Or more singing: 'My feet are here on Broadway …'

'ONE VOICE!'

Rain

We stood straight as anything outside Granny's house. She had died, but people gathered because she had lived, and we were proud to have known her. There is a great relief in Ireland when someone dies – you can then lavish on them all the praise and expressions of love that you couldn't extend to them while still alive. If you told Granny that you loved her while she was still living, you'd be liable to get a nip and told not to be using idle language like that. Not that anyone in our house was ever going to mention love to Granny or anyone else. Pointing words like that at someone only disturbed them and weakened their trust. Best to talk about the lovely teapot or the dainty wee cups or the new jug.

Granny was eighty-nine but claimed to be ninety – thought she'd get extra sympathy for being ninety. But her death only caused the normal amount of grief and fuss. They said she was ready to go. That she had had a good life. These assumptions were based on the extraordinary amount of bingo she had got through in her later years. But she was born in 1896 or 1897. What she did between then and the 1970s, when the bingo craze started, seemed to be forgotten. No one remembered or mentioned her early life – the poverty – the unfortunate fate of being from Drumreilly or her arranged marriage to a dimlick of a farmer from over the fields. The seven children one after the other and her husband's constant yearning for books and playing the fiddle. And most of all, the missing 'O' from his family name. She did manage to reintroduce the 'O' in the late forties ... went to America to one of her daughters and wrote home to Michael O'Rourke, Drumshangore, Carrigallen, County Leitrim. That let everyone know that we were now the 'O'Rourkes' and not the duck-shit Rourkes of before. 'Standing' was important to the old people, and my granny had it in bucketfuls. There's still a bit of it in us. Some of us. Not the most likeable quality – but it's there. Still the auld want in us.

I had never seen my father cry ... and Mammy wasn't far behind him. Some women were always crying, but not Mammy. She kept the waterworks for when she was making a bargain in Mullen market, or buying shoes in Ballinamore. If she thought crying might get her a few pence off the price, then she could cry like anything. But in general, she found a way around the tears. That gave her great consistency as a mother. And with Daddy's sensible take on everything – except football – we grew up in an environment of fully bolted down emotion.

Granny died on the 15th of July 1986 – St Swithin's Day. The weather on St Swithin's Day predicts the weather for the next 40 days. It rained that day. On Thursday, the 17th of July, the main protagonists at Granny's wake finally emerged from the corpse room on Boley Hill. Six of Granny's children had said their final goodbyes. My aunt Vera, whom I never met, didn't travel home for the funeral, but my father and Michael and Father Kevin, along with Peggy, Monica and Theresa, were all present and suitably sad. Granny wouldn't want gushes of tears – tears were for common-ers and pathetic when laid on too thick. So red eyes and glum faces were the order of the day. My father and Peggy were always laid back. Michael and his re-oc-curring enthusiasm took its toll. Aunt Monica was a swanky clone of her mother, while Father Kevin was a paradox of spirituality and common sense. My mad aunt Theresa was a born-again Christian – heavy on the spiritual without any common sense. She had neither penny nor care in the world and was just as liable to burst into song as she was to recite her latest poem.

A romantic who never found romance ... a homebird who never could find home. She had poetry published in Washington – exaggerated words of love for green hills and whitewashed walls and ladeens walking down every boreen. An Ireland for Americans: nothing like the real Ireland with the new silage and the rain.

The rain didn't start on St Swithin's Day that year. It had been raining already – raining from the year before. And it continued for 40 days and nights and more because '86 was another '85 – wet and grey – perfect for grief and misery and putting out buckets to catch the drop.

At Granny's burial in Drumeela, my aunt Theresa sang 'How Great Thou Art'. Her sweet voice rang out among the mourners at the graveside – her romantic green hills almost meeting her halfway. It was perfect, even with the rain. There is great power in unaccompanied song. It takes great courage to sing alone. Right throughout her life, my aunt Theresa sang alone – she brought great joy to others as she sang away her pain.

There was a procession of visitors for a long time after Granny died. My mother's nerves on tenterhooks – listening out for cars and strange noises. Mammy could smell a visitor a mile off.

'Friggers of visitors and nothing in the house. What's taking them? How long are they going to stay?'

The number of times I came home in 1986 to find some strange little man and his big lorryload of a wife sitting up at our kitchen table eating feeds of ham and lettuce and salad cream. Big jowls munching and regurgitating, smacking lips and sporadic muttering about such a one, who lives in such a lane, past so and so, near the bad turn … and that their cousin in Lanesboro caught his mickey in a cracked flowerpot. And the dangers of cracked flowerpots and living in Lanesboro and walking about with your mickey hanging out. And these visitors went on and on and on – went on even longer than the rain. And my poor grieving father would sit there and say, 'Mmmmm …' and 'That's a sight …' and him with no more interest in these bloody visitors and their ability to sabotage the existence of most human forms. Was it any wonder my mother was paranoid?

I went to visit Granny once – independently – as an adult – without reminder or persuasion. She wasn't expecting me, but without anyone else present, she took in her horns of pride and misplaced judgement. She was an all-right sort, not as blunt and all-knowing as I was expecting. Just an old woman trying to put right her past indiscretions. So that's what we do? Blunder our way through life, knocking over everything around us, and then when it's almost too late, we start to tidy up.

I didn't ask her about her youth or what made her so driven – so devoid of flexibility. I just mentioned the nice teapot, the dainty cups and the lovely tea. Maybe we can communicate in roundabout dialogue? I don't think so. All I remember of her was her cheeks and her astonishment at our ability to speak out of turn. And she hated daisies, used to pour boiling water on them when they infiltrated her tiny lawn. What a waste of hot water, and her with such a lovely teapot.

As the second year of persistent rain, 1986 was another year of silage entanglements. I'm sure at the time we thought the climate was broken, that we'd never see another sunny day ... but we did. Rain is so often the curse of western farming, but it has its moments. Sometimes – and they were few and far between – in August or September when we were bringing in the hay on one of our tiny outlying farms, I'd see the clouds gathering – wonder was there a chance that the rain might come on. We'd work like the divil till one o'clock and then Mammy would come with tea and bread and an assortment of fillings – ham and eggs, onion and salad cream – and we'd set up café in the half empty hayshed and eat. We never talked much, apart from what was done and what was to be done. And always – will the rain hold off? And sometimes when the gods in heaven

were aligned, they'd send drops of rain. One at a time
at first and then in pairs ... and one and two, and so
the tune would begin. The sound of rain on the tin roof
will always comfort me. Work, and the rush to get back
to it, would be suspended and we'd lie back in the hay
and listen. My father and mother, and probably my
brother, were listening, hoping it was only a shower –
I was praying for a downpour. I wanted the rhythm of
the drops on the roof to be matched by the dancing
splashes on the street – jumping fountains of water and
the tiny rivers channelling through dry mud on the floor
of the shed. Play for me a symphony of rain.

My aunts and uncles stayed for a few days after
Granny's funeral. For the first time I caught a glimpse
of my father's family as a family and not as individuals scattered far and wide. They made easy watching.
A lightness that I hadn't seen before. Theresa leading the
way with poems and songs; Michael, not to be outdone,
with his own renditions; and Father Kevin leaning heavy
on the mug for the right note. Monica was more tactful,
graceful with a hint of Granny in her tail. She came up
with the titles, but I never heard her sing. My father
thought he'd get away with being his usual steady self,
but even he was dragged back into being one of them –
and he sang. Without the showmanship of the others;

his song was quiet and, yes, steady – but still, the hoor could sing.

My mother grinded hard in the kitchen, left no one without a cup or glass or knife and fork in their hand. She had her own magic way of staying well clear of the limelight ... a limelight that some of the others so desperately craved. The younger generation were not called upon to entertain. My sister Geraldine could sing – fill the house with sultry tones as she washed the dishes. And I had sung a few times – in secluded places or in the byre. In fact, we all sang in the byre – the milking machine surrounding the bum notes with a satin shield. The pop tunes rang out: Rod Stewart's 'Do Ya Think I'm Sexy'. The audience, left spellbound, and chewing their cud.

The talent show

We were lined up – three in front of four. I was at the back on the left wing. We were the Drumeela Macra na Feirme ballad group and Tommy Brady was our conductor. Tommy Brady epitomised everything that was good about Macra. A quiet shell of a young fella, who grew through the organisation, learned skills, took responsibility ... gained in confidence and blossomed into a right capable young man. He hadn't a note in his head, but he was the chairman – our leader – and he led from the front. Tonight we were practising for the talent competition – talent in its broadest sense. Drumeela, Fenagh and Aughnasheelin would battle it out in Aughnasheelin Hall for the un-coveted prize of being Leitrim Macra na Feirme talent competition champions. The competition consisted of ballad group singing, solo singing, sketches, instrumental music and a question time. Not many of our crowd excelled in any of the aforementioned – but like our chairman, we had developed the neck to take on whatever popped up in front of us. Not always a good thing.

It's a funny word, 'talent' – it gets bandied about a lot these days. Along with words like 'genius' and 'legend'. But I must tell you that there was a time – like in October 1986 – when there wasn't a genius or legend to be found in Newtowngore. Now they're all over the place. The other thing we were missing as we practised for the upcoming talent competition was talent. None of us had it – not even the hidden variety. We had youth and an abundance of sheer neck – but without talent, there was a fair chance that we'd be found out unless the other participants were just as bad or worse.

Pat Bradley was our main hope in the solo singing. His unaccompanied version of 'Patricia the Stripper' was downright sexy and with certain farming connotations thrown in, he milked it for all he was worth. Someone could play the tin whistle and that was the instrumental category taken care of. There were loads of know-it-alls available, so the question time team was laden down with knowledge and speculation. The sketch section was, as yet, sketchy, but the ballad group was the crème de la crème under the supervision of our tone-deaf supervisor.

'Step away from the group, Seamus,' I was told in no uncertain terms as my voice layered beautifully upon the others – the order coming from our imperious leader himself, Tommy 'No Shit' Brady.

'I beg your pardon' is what I should have said, but I didn't. I froze, getting redder by the second. My Macra development was not as far on as I had thought.

'You just sound like shite,' Tommy exultantly explained. 'You sound like a foghorn, Seamus. Step away and we'll see if it makes any difference.'

And I did. And it did. And that was it. Seven became six and the ballad group was nailed down – or should have been. What was I going to do so?

'You might come up with a sketch, Seamus.' And that was everything in the talent competition taken care of. But it wasn't. I had been handed something that I hadn't a clue about! But sure, what odds? I stirred up whatever neck I had left and began the sketch. The scene would take place in a pub – I would be the publican in charge. Mary Lynch would be my wife. I was liking the dramatic licence to pick and choose what went on in this fabricated world – a lot easier than having to deal with what was happening in my real world.

My real world was devoid of anything dramatic, except disappointment and despair, and rejection and jilted romance and tainted love and pent-up desire, followed by a series of beautiful bad thoughts! How could you put that into a Macra na Feirme sketch? Mary Lynch thought I was slightly overthinking it and I was. My ability to think outside the box, even before we had a box, was remarkable. We came up with a sketch about a pub that was having a talent competition. How off the charts was that? We didn't bother with a script, we said we'd make it up as we went along. That was very … very … interesting …

By the end of that October, Macra and our dabbling in show business were all I could look forward to. I was tired of commuting 40 minutes each way to work that I hated. I never enjoyed being available for farmwork in the evenings or at the weekends. Football was a hardship. Dieting and eating my troubles away weren't bearing any success. I was, once again, longing to get away from what I came back to. 'A pure sign of an eejit,' as my father explained! He had watched my journey through all the phases of being an eejit – so he knew.

When I was in America, the Leitrim county board had promised to help find me a job back in Ireland. That was if I couldn't find one myself. It was a carrot to entice me back to play football. Maybe it was time to call in this offer. Any job would be better than what I had. I made enquiries. Dublin was mentioned. Dublin was perfect. There was a perceived glamour about ones working in Dublin. Coming back at the weekends like film stars. Oh, to be working in Dublin. Away but not away. Home, but not at home. You could have sex in Dublin. There were couples from home living together in Dublin. Red-raw from sex and staying up late! And when they'd come home at the weekend, it'd be back to him picking her up at eight and bringing her home before one – the parents knowing full well what was going on in the city. But as long as it wasn't happening on their own doorstep, they could ride away good-o. Of course, at twenty-one, the term 'living together' didn't make much sense. How would you fill your time after the sex and the staying up late?

I got a call to go to a woodworking shop off Gardiner Street. Irish Woodworking Ltd was a Dublin company looking for cabinet makers. I gathered up my certificates and heavy coat and drove to Dublin. I met Mr Foley and his son. I had never called anyone 'mister' before, but Mr Foley was a nice soft-spoken man. Was it possible that the boss of any company could be nice? As it turned out, it was! I got my start date. Enough time to break up with my current employer and find somewhere to live.

Bedsits were ten a penny at the time. Twenty pounds for a ground floor flat on the North Circular

Road – shared toilet and shower, walk-in bedroom-cum-kitchen-cum-lounge – 12x10 luxury living for the culchies. It was perfect. All I had to do now was nail this sketch for the talent competition.

I had a certain amount of nervousness running through me as I looked down from the stage in Aughnasheelin Hall. It was an hour before curtain. I didn't know what I was doing – I had never been on a stage before. If I had any experience of what was to come, I would have been far more nervous. What possessed me? I was quickly becoming aware that the moment I walked out onto these boards – this platform – I'd better have something to show for myself. I remembered going to Carrigallen Hall to watch the Carrigallen Community Players. I remembered the magic of the curtains opening and the scenes unfolding. How could I be so slack as to be roped into this? Macra na Feirme had always been looked upon as a second-rate organisation for nitwit farmers and gobshites. And we had proved that to be wrong when we organised the ploughing match and the summer festival and instigated help for struggling farmers during the wet years of '85 and '86. But going out on stage to perform a sketch with no script was going to bring us right back to being gobshites and nitwits.

I cannot describe that night in November '86 – my first time on stage. It's too embarrassing – the stuff of nightmares. Thankfully, there weren't many to see it. But I learned a valuable lesson. Never ever take going on stage lightly. The most dangerous thing on earth if not treated with the utmost respect. It will never be all right on the night, unless you have planned and practised and carefully prepared. Otherwise, you might get your head taken off.

I moved into my new bedsit in Dublin. It was snug. A week later, I got a call from my county mate Donie McLoughlin. He was back from New York and starting work in Dublin. Was there room on my horse for two? He moved in with immediate effect. Now we were even more snug.

Dublin was great, but not as sexy as I had hoped. Work started at eight, finished at six – the flat was full of sawdust. The dinner was made on the frying pan – the room diminishing daily. There was a housemate, a housemate's sleeping bag and a large pile of fermenting socks and underwear waiting for Mammy's washing machine at the weekend. Then there was a call from another county colleague, Brendan Conway. He needed a place – just for a few days! And then there were three. Three big sweaty men in a small bedsit took its toll, but it was cheap – and empty at the weekends. We always went home at the weekend. There was always a match at home or an important social gathering. An opportunity to parade yourself up for Communion because you were now working in Dublin. And we got our washing done – otherwise we'd have to buy more essentials in Dunnes Stores. And on Sunday night, we went to Mohill to a disco. Not home till four in the morning, set off again at six to head back to Dublin via Cloone and Fenagh and pick up Brendan Conway, Donie McLoughlin and any stragglers who might have missed the bus.

Work on Monday was rest from socialising and driving and eating. We ate all we could at home and brought back homemade bread and the leftover Sunday roast. And the clean clothes and maybe a houseplant or two that my mother sent, thinking they might be nice in our overcrowded abode in Dublin 7. There was little enough oxygen as it was.

Life and death

I had a Drumreilly girlfriend. I wasn't proud of it; it just happened. It wasn't love at first sight. It was love after several sightings and misunderstandings and 'does she really fancy me' and playing hard to get and playing hurt and most of the time playing football against her parish, or half-parish, Drumreilly. And me a kind of a half Drumreilly man myself. But she was lovely. Lilly.

There's a theory that the ones from the neighbouring parishes are probably very like ourselves. If that's true, then the theory that we often hate ourselves is also true. We hated Drumreilly – not the individuals, although some of the individuals were hard work, but we hated the concept of these prehistoric mammals getting the better of us on a football field. Even my mother prayed that we'd hammer seven kinds of shite out of Drumreilly. And she had no interest in football – never went to a match in her life. But picking up the pieces after a defeat to our neighbours was not time well spent. And it was her who would have to deal with the big sulk after such losses. My father analysing away in the corner, bringing it back to lack of effort or 'too many late nights', or worse still, 'cockiness'.

In the '80s, defeats against Drumreilly were minimal. For a few short years, we had bragging rights – not that we bragged or boasted. That would be childish, and anyway, there was always the fear that the winning streak might come to an end. In December of '86 we were down to play Drumreilly in a Division 2 league final. Nothing would stop us – not fear, not cockiness, not girlfriends. Nothing. How could we face Christmas and all the pampering that goes with that, if we couldn't beat Drumreilly? We left no stone unturned.

Meanwhile, my life in Dublin was remarkably boring. The money wasn't great, and although rent was cheap, it was hard to have money for anything. Running out of money was a bump in the road that I hadn't had to contend with before. I always had money. Not lots but enough. But Dublin was hard on money, and driving up and down at the weekends, and the cost of living – or the cost of living it up – had me stretched. So much so that one Thursday evening, instead of going out, we went to a mission. Me and Donie McLoughlin and Brendan Conway headed off to Finglas where Father

Michael Cleary was giving a mission – or whatever they did with missions. Father Michael was a celebrity at the time – the Singing Priest. A charismatic man who you'd nearly go to see even if you had money to go somewhere else. He gave religion a relevance that we hadn't been aware of before, and it was good craic! A handy way of putting in an evening on the dry. Father Cleary was later reported to have had a family with his housekeeper – maybe that's what gave him his relevance. He talked that night about the preciousness of life. Not about how we lived our lives, but the will to live it, to survive. He said he was working with people at the time who were only a breath away from death. Think about that. Hard for big hardy footballers, even Leitrim footballers, to fathom what that was like.

The game against Drumreilly was foremost on my mind.

'Oh God, don't let the Drumreillys beat yez,' my mother had said.

There were rumours that Drumreilly were horrid fit – frog-jumping around their new pitch in Carrickmakeegan. I laughed at the image, but it was no laughing matter.

'Wait till Michael Maguire leaps across you and away up the field,' my father pointed out.

'But they're hardly going to frog-jump during the game …?'

'Don't be so cocky!' I was told. My father didn't mind sounding ridiculous as long as he got his point across. Like when I suggested changing my car. He couldn't help himself from pointing out that if I was to get a new car, he'd have to get used to it being parked at the front of the house; just like he had to get used to the last one being parked there. Reversed into it several times before the penny eventually dropped that there was a car. And what did I need a change of car for anyway?

I said, 'To get from A to B.'

That set him off completely. 'What are you talking about A to B? Sure there's no such place as A and why would you be there in the first place, let alone wanting to head off for B. Where is B, no more than A?' And he went on and on, pretending to be stupid as fuck – and him not one bit stupid. But he knew I had no money, and we were as well arguing over As and Bs as him pointing out the real facts. Which he was well capable of too – but the real facts might hurt a little too much. So he just played the ridiculous.

The morning of the big game, I headed to Mullen market to take my mind off the impending battle. I drove over past Drumeela church and school, on to

Taaffe's Cross. That time Taaffe's Cross was a straightforward crossroads. A stop sign on the Drumeela side,
but not many of us smart fellas stopped at the stop sign.
You could see for a good distance either side, so most
just slowed down, and if there was nothing coming, we
gave her the diddy and away like hell down the mountain road. Even at night, the stop sign wasn't a problem
because switching off your headlights for a few seconds
as you approached a junction was a newfangled way
of detecting oncoming traffic at the time. It became so
popular that cars from both sides were doing it ... which
resulted in a spate of crashes, with both vehicles unlit at
the moment of impact. My father was one of the first to
point out the failings of the 'turning off your headlights'
method. 'What's their hurry?' he'd say, and of course,
as usual, he was right.

I wasn't one for taking chances. I headed through
Taaffe's Cross – down the mountain road, till I came
to Fartrin Cross. This time I had the right of way, but
I was in the habit of slowing down here too, because
often cars from the Ardlougher side thought they had
the right of way. And also, because there was a cloud
of dust hanging at Fartrin Cross. A car with three passengers had driven straight across the main road and hit
an army jeep coming from Ballyconnell. The jeep was

upside down and the car had sped into the ditch out of sight. I was the first on the scene.

I stopped and ran to the jeep. A young army officer was getting to his feet after extracting himself from the wreck; another started roaring that there was battery acid dripping on him. Another was unconscious. Then I saw the car. The top seemed to have been sheared off it. I tried to help the ones screaming the most, but they were all trapped. I needed to get help and fast. There were no mobile phones; it was up to me to get help. I jumped into my car and headed for Ballyconnell Garda station. I remember thinking, *this is why I need a new car*, I couldn't get it to go quick enough. Eventually, I got to the station and ran inside and blurted that there was after being a serious accident. I thought they'd come running, but they wanted to know my name and where I was from ... and all this time there were lives at stake – people only a breath away from death.

'Please call the ambulance and the fire brigade. Please help!' And they did – eventually.

Three people died in the crash. When I got back to the scene, there were blue lights flashing and lots of onlookers, lots of experts on what had happened. Then, there was silence ... as the seriousness of it all set in. God has a way of calling us to order, silencing our silly human gabbling. We're great at making noise. We don't like the silence of death. And I tell this story because it fell before our big game, because it put our local rivalry in the shade. Up until then, playing Drumreilly was a matter of life and death. I discovered it was only a matter of life and the tiny shifts within it. Death was a different thing altogether. I didn't know any of the deceased, where they were going or what their plans were for that dreary Sunday. I felt hollow and spent. Not the way to approach an important football match.

By the time I got to Fenagh, I had forgotten what these games meant to our two half-parishes. The roads lined – the car park full. Car doors opening – legs thrown out on gravel and tar – shuffling shoes searching for traction. More arms appearing – crippled hands clutching on car door handles – the scramble for elevation. Like the maternity ward of a scrap heap, old men and women were pushed out among the angst and the deliberation. Coughing and spluttering and crying out, 'Up Drumreilly!'

'Come on, Carrigallen!'

'We have yez the year.'

'Yez have nothing, only wet bad fields.'

'Shut up, Mac, or I'll break your jaw.'

And so it went on – and that was only the supporters.

I must have been quiet. Someone said, 'Are ya all right?' and I said, 'Aye.' And that was it. I didn't tell anyone where I'd been or what I had seen. I just hid behind the bravado of youth and togged out and ran out and didn't try to make sense of what was going on. There was the usual snarling and pushing before the game, and I found comfort in that. Delighted to be able to feel it, see it, hear it – the honour of being able to live it. There was a vicious row in the second half – lads ran in from the sidelines, fences were jumped, and flag-poles used as batons. One famous umbrella was stuck up where there was no rain. It was a scandal; the talk of the country for days. Who hit who and who was the woman with the umbrella? And, best of all, the game was a draw, and so it would all be happening again very, very soon.

Home for the holidays

I had changed my car. What a stupid thing to do! I now had a loan as well as having no money. And I bought a Toyota Corolla – a beige one – the most uncool, nondescript car you could have at the time. Your man in the garage said that it had been owned by a widow woman. Obviously widows were easy on cars. There was small mileage on it – clearly a widow who didn't go anywhere. I had built my driving reputation on having a red sporty car, all chrome and straightened-out bumpers. The Auld Lad reversing into it at every opportunity. A car with stubble, that's what it was – not a watery auld soft-faced car like this Toyota. What was I thinking?

It was coming up to Christmas '86. A good time for 21-year-olds. We had beaten Drumreilly in the replay. I was one of the stars. Well, even my Auld Lad said, 'And you weren't as bad as I often saw ya.' That had to stand for something. I went out in Dublin to celebrate. We went to O'Donoghue's pub up near St Stephen's

Green. 'A significant drinking establishment,' I was told – home to the Dubliners when they were starting out. Sounded like a good place to start drinking properly. I was drinking a while at this stage, but not properly. Not that I could mention how many pints I had. I only ever had three or four. That wasn't good enough. I had drunk a good few bottles of Bud when I was in America, but that was on my own, and I didn't know how much I drank, only that the songs written on the jukebox were duplicated, and I had to close one eye to choose and put in my quarter. Or another time when I stumbled onto the dancefloor of a Manhattan bar and started snogging this young one that was eying me up. And when we finished snogging, we realised that neither of us could talk, we were that drunk. But apart from that, I didn't drink much. And I wasn't setting out to be a drinker – I just wanted this night to be about good pints of Guinness and acting like a grown-up. I brought Messrs McLoughlin and Conway with me – that didn't up the maturity – and we ordered three pints. And then three pints ... and three pints more ... And off took my drinking career! Apparently, the Guinness was lovely, and I took to it like a suck calf. The pub closed at closing time, and we walked home, delighted with ourselves. The next day was my last day at work before Christmas. I was now a bona fide Dublin-based Guinness-drinking Division 2 league medal holder, and I drove home the next day with an acceptable amount of joy and alcohol in my veins.

On Christmas night, I went to the Sportsman in Mohill – to the disco – and because it was Christmas night the bar didn't open till midnight. Fair enough. I didn't need drink. I was glowing enough from my recent sporting achievements. Women kept looking over. It was amazing. I stood with my back to the bar, 7UP in hand, and everyone was looking over. Yes, the women, but the men too. They couldn't help but admire the fine specimen that I was. I had new 501 jeans. I had big American runners and a polo-neck black shirt. And to go with that, I had a white shoulder-padded jacket with the buttons going diagonally across my chest – a bit of a George Michael look. I was loving the attention. I was weighing up my options. Stay where I was and avoid disappointment – which was never a bad option – or go for one of these chicks? There were no stand-out beauties, but they were all looking over. I turned around to the bar to gain more composure, and as I straightened myself, I could see this big wall clock above my head.

That's what they were looking at! Not me. Not my physique. Not my mesmerising fashion sense. They were watching the clock creep towards midnight. They were waiting for the bar to open! I was very put out. I drank my 7UP and with a shrug of my padded shoulders I found a place to sit. I saw Lilly from Drumreilly. We were no longer an item. Not because of the football, but because she had discovered that I was a bit of a bollix. How she discovered that, I don't know!

I still wasn't great at relationships – they seemed a bit pointless. I'll pick you up at eight and we'll go here or there, and we'll be boyfriend and girlfriend. Driving about with a live hand grenade in your trousers – and the length of some of the lanes. Then, a bit of nookie outside her house before she went to bed and you went off home to your bed – your artillery firmly tucked away between your legs. I wasn't able for all that. And although tonight had flattered to deceive, it might improve. *Wait till the bar opens and they start drinking. They might be compelled to look over again.*

I never liked the Sportsman in Mohill – not compelling enough. The second night of Christmas would be different. St Stephen's night I would go to Carrigallen – to the hotel – and what the Kilbrackan Arms lacked in imagination it made up for in madness. It was beaming in the glow of Christmas and our recent win in the football. Pat Magee bought me a pint, and apart from dodgy

bumper repairs, Pat Magee was one of our most knowl-
edgeable exponents of GAA negativity in the parish. He,
like my father, knew how bad I could be. So when he
said, 'You don't often deserve it, but I think you deserve
a pint for beatin' that crowd,' that was it – the night
was off to a flyer! There was a dance in the function
room. Yes, a parish dance, but a dance that would keep
the bar open. Closing times were important back then.
John Mulligan, our local sergeant, was a rash on the
town's arse for keeping closing time. A man possessed
by the tail end of a clock. Once it got near closing time,
whatever he was doing, he'd reinvigorate himself into
his uniform and away down the town, listening out
for people enjoying themselves. Then, just as Dougie
Stewart or Tim Mulligan were loosening the nuts on the
high notes of 'I'll Take You Home Again, Kathleen' or
'Nessun Dorma', the sergeant would slide in under the
door and stand there with his torch and his notebook,
and the tongue hanging out of his mouth, ready to lick
the pencil. Such a hoor for turning up and walking in.
And then the little cough ... He was a nice man – a man
you could talk to – secretary of the football club and the
tug of war club and on the bingo committee. But whatever it was to him and this thing of doing his job, you
just couldn't trust him.

Thankfully, he was off duty that night, him and the wife dancing away above in the function room. The band was cat, but any band would take up the slack at a dance the second night of Christmas. It was all good craic. The footballers were there, recounting classic encounters of Leitrim Junior and Division 2 football. The Macra na Feirme crowd, fresh from their victory in the Leitrim Macra na Feirme talent competition. My second cousin Geraldine Mimna was there, horsin' drink into me and telling me I was no craic. She was great craic – always with a broad smile and the big infectious laugh. The best of company always. And I don't know about her, but I was starting to close one eye in order to see out of the other.

Pat Bradley grabbed the microphone and began a rendition of his number one Macra na Feirme solo singing hit 'Patricia the Stripper'. The band were tagging along and everyone was singing, and what did I go and do? Some demon caught a hold of me, and I sprang to my feet like a frog-jumpin' Drumreilly footballer and started to reenact the shameful case of Patricia, otherwise known as 'Delicia', taking off all her clothes. '*And with a swing of her hips, she started to strip …*' I started to dance and strip – top half only – and everyone was laughing and cheering. The more serious I was, the more they laughed, and myself and Pat Bradly milked 'Patricia the Stripper' for all she was worth. And drunk as I was at the time, I discovered something for myself. If you could keep Sergeant Mulligan out of his uniform, the craic would be endless.

I was fairly tender the next morning. I had let out a bundle of farts during the night that affected my brother's sleep. Firstly by the noise and secondly by the lasting pungent fragrance. He had tried to shake me, but that only stirred more of the aroma, and so he got up and milked early. When I got up and entered the kitchen, everyone was having another Christmas breakfast. I knew that word of my impromptu performance had already hit the family airwaves, as there was a great sense of sadness and bewilderment as I sat down to my sausages. What had I done? I had made a complete holy show of myself and my family in front of the whole town of Carrigallen, including the sergeant and Pat Magee and God knows who else was lying under a table drunk or shielding their eyes from such promiscuity. And in Harte's hotel – the Kilbrackan Arms – where Mammy and Geraldine worked at weddings and dinner dances. What if it had been a dinner dance and my mother had caught sight of me from the kitchen – her favourite son – her poor innocent little boy – that she had plucked from the jaws of death when I fell into the bog hole that time in 1969? What if she saw me gyrating and grinding up against Mrs Flemming and Mrs Sheridan – Cathal Sheridan's mother. Nothing good would come out of dancing and laughing and actin' the goat. No one said a word – they didn't have to. I ate my breakfast and planned my return to Harte's hotel that night. It had something that I was searching for.

The art of eating

The bedsit on the North Circular Road was a kip – not because of the landlord or the council or the government, but because three boys from Leitrim didn't do any dusting or tidying or washing. We were waiting for the maid who never came. It became a health issue. There were fungi living in the lap of luxury in our flat, while we were gasping for air and some personal space. The daily paper was purchased, and we searched for a house or a half a house for three. *The entire first floor of a contemporary Drumcondra dwelling* was circled in pen. It sounded beyond us – but it was on Richmond Road, and it was £45 per week. The thought of living in a contemporary anything sounded classy. We met the landlord there to have a look around. He was a builder from Offaly and the flat was as contemporary as our auld scullery at home. It had three small bedrooms, a three-cornered sitting room and a kitchen the size of a large walk-in press. We took it. 'Fuck it,' we said. It was beside Croke Park – crucial for three Leitrim footballers at the time – and it was also near the main strip of culchie pubs on Dorset Street and the Drumcondra Road.

The other thing was that St Pat's teacher training college was just over the road and there were three young women who studied there living downstairs. Now, they were contemporary and giggly and there were wafts of lovely girls coming up the stairs as we moved in one Monday evening. This could be it. This could be the making of us – of me. My people and my people's people would be proud to know that I was now living above three teachers.

I was conscious of my common qualities – my large thick agricultural head, my big hands and my sloping walk. I hadn't improved myself by going all George Michael and Spandau Ballet and dressing out of Mullen market. It was time to buck up. I'd soon be twenty-two. I bought myself a long heavy coat and scarf. That was a good move. I now looked like a doctor or a gynaecologist – as long as I kept my hands in my pockets. I also decided to stay in Dublin for a weekend. There was a rugby match in Lansdowne Road. Ireland were playing France, and I had a ticket. We had met the girls from downstairs. They seemed okay. I immediately fell in love with one of them, and the other two were lovely too.

But the one I fancied had let it slip that she was staying up for that same weekend. She was from Westmeath. I thought she'd have been from somewhere sexier than Mullingar, but maybe there was a posh part I hadn't heard about. They weren't overly impressed with our Leitrim connections either, which did cause some early friction. But they could all tell by my coat that I was ready to launch into a contemporary love affair. All I needed was some time alone with this one girl – time to Dublinise myself.

I had tried to Dublinise myself a few months before – started to visit my relations in Clontarf, but it didn't end well. My mother's cousin Rosaleen and her Cork husband, Dick, were the embodiment of fun and laughter. Rosaleen had been like a sister to my mother growing up and they remained extremely close. Their kids, Ita, Sara and John, had spent summers with us on the farm in Leitrim – making hay; going to the bog; milking cows. They were a tonic! We were fierce fond of them. They were younger than us, but never failed to lift our gloomy spirits.

As part of my development plan when I went to Dublin first, I drove out to the Stiles Road to visit these lofty cousins and to somehow Dublinise myself. Shake off the cows' cleanins and splatters of muck, and

somehow straighten myself up. Rosaleen was a wonderfully decent Cavan woman and had the same motto as
my mother: 'Feed first, ask questions later.' The kettle
was put on, and after what seemed like only minutes, a
feed was set before me: a fry – a moderate fry, I would
call it – two sausages, two slices of bacon, an egg, black
and white pudding. Moderate but more than enough for
a lad after eating his dinner. The youngsters, Ita, Sara
and John, took up ringside seats to watch me eating.

This entertainment had originated in Drumshangore
when they were on their holidays. They thought that
the spectacle of me and my brother eating was one of
the wonders of the world. They used to get up early
to watch my brother, Kevin, eat his porridge. I would
hear howls of laughter coming from the kitchen at 6.30
in the morning. They'd be cheering every mouthful –
the hand-eye coordination; the size of the spoonfuls;
the speed of the refill; the catching of the drip; and the
eventual look of contentment when he threw the empty
saucepan in the sink. They thought we were savages, in
the best possible sense. In the evenings, their attraction
to our eating would move to the dinner table. The highlight – watching Kevin eating his dinner while nodding
off to sleep. A hard watch. Kevin was an unbelievable
worker. He got more hardship around that farm from

6.30 a.m. till midnight doing the things. And he was prone to falling asleep.

Sometimes we'd watch from the kitchen window as Kevin topped the rushes in the field behind the house. Once a sequence of small fields, it was now a five-acre arena for 'mowing while sleeping'. The monotony of going round and round in circles for so long used to send Kevin dozing, and he'd be there with his head hanging out the door of the tractor, a zigzag pattern behind him as the steering wheel shifted with every hump and bump. And Mammy'd say, 'I hope that fella wakes up before his dinner.'

And then at dinner, with our cousins in position, the headline event would commence. My dear brother would drive the fork into the pile of spuds and lift. Then there would be a wobble – a tiredness coming over him as his eyelids began to slide shut. At the same time, the forkful of spuds would begin to lose altitude, but with a sudden pang of hunger, the fork would again gain elevation to a level three-quarter ways up to his chin. A brief moment of rest ... and then ... pop goes the weasel! With a swift intake of breath, the spuds were sucked into the mouth and swallowed whole, leaving only a small portion of the fork-handle exposed. But, with the precision of a surgeon, the fork was then extracted from the mouth, and with a shiver of intent, the harrowing routine would be repeated.

Kevin often spent an hour eating his dinner, as sleep deprivation was so prevalent, especially during the wet years of '85 and '86. But me and Kevin both knew we could eat a good dinner in two and a half minutes flat if we avoided chit-chat and the passing of the brown sauce. These demonstrations of savagery were a great source of pride and entertainment to our cousins in Dublin, and when I sat down to dine with them, they were riveted.

I ate my fry-up as politely as I could – only extracting the odd titter from the three. We all chatted about my hectic life in Dublin, and they said to call soon again. I did. This time the fry was increased by about 15 per cent, because they thought I hadn't got enough to eat the last time. There was more of everything, with a bit of liver thrown in for health reasons. It was too much, but our family were never known to leave anything on the plate. That would be an insult. But by eating everything, poor Rosaleen thought I was being under-fed. And so, when I returned a third time, my portions were up 23 per cent, plus chips and chicken nuggets. This would be a challenge, but a challenge I was up to. But when I called a fourth time, with two plates now taking the place of one and with mushrooms and hash-browns now added to the menu, it was time to shut off relationships with my relations. I couldn't possibly eat any more, and yet, I couldn't possibly leave anything behind me. In simple terms, I would never fit in among the superior classes.

My weekend in our Richmond Road accommodation was going great. I had brought my long coat and scarf out for a walk, and I even met Carol, the girl I fancied, as I returned. She said, 'Call in any time.' And I said, 'Likewise.' I went upstairs and waited, but she didn't come. I was hungry. I put on the pan. A lorry load of pork frying like billy-o on the pan – and this was before extractor fans and smoke alarms. I was going to have a good feed before I went to the rugby, and I liked everything well done: the sausages, the bacon, the pudding, the lamb chops and the fish fingers. A gentle smog hung over me as I tended my creation. I had removed my shirt, so it wouldn't get ruined by the odd spit from the chops landing on my chest. And then the phone rang in the hall downstairs. Then a knock on my kitchen door. It was her – Carol! I was not in a position to accept visitors!

'Yes?' I said.

'Can I come in?'

I turned off the pan. The smoke was now hurting my eyes. I quickly put on my big coat to cover my naked chest. You could still see my chest.

'Are you okay?' Carol enquired. It was so nice of her to ask.

'Yeah. Just a sec.'

I opened the door. Carol stood there – full of light air, ready to flirt her way into my cosmos – to tell me that the phone was just her mother, and to hope that it didn't bother me. And isn't it so wonderfully weird that we were thrown together for the weekend in the same house ... alone ... and yet together. But she didn't say that. She said nothing. She just stood there with a strange look on her face. And I had seen that look before. A look of disappointment and fear. Here was a man, with the reddest face and the heaviest coat and no shirt and a stack of cremated meat on the pan. That could only mean one thing. I was a flasher and a murderer and probably a cannibal to boot – cooking the chopped-up body parts of my latest victim. And that I was not to be trusted. Or snogged. Or brought home to Mullingar.

Help

It was a Thursday night in Dublin. I was in Grogan's pub on South William Street. I slid my hand around the sides of a pint. Not in any great hurry to drink it. Not in any hurry to do anything. I had gone with a work-mate for two pints, and we had drunk them and now he was gone. Paddy Hayes from Terenure was like that. He would do exactly as he had said. A good trait in a lad! Our boss, Mr Foley, liked that in his staff. He liked it in me too. I was like that at work. If I said I'd do it, I did. 'Do it and be done with it,' my father used to say. And he was right. But doing it was one thing – making the decision to do it was another. Decision-making is vital. Even a wrong decision can get things done – whereas pondering will get you nowhere. And being twenty-one in 1986 was a ponderer's paradise. Apart from work, I'd spend half my time sitting on the fence and the other half mulling over what might have been.

I had made arrangements to meet a girl in Rathmines on that same Thursday night. I had also agreed to meet an ex of mine on O'Connell Street, and at the same time, I had promised a third to go to the cinema. These were three different women that I was supposed to be meeting, but I wasn't going anywhere just yet. I have an agreeable nature. Someone would suggest meeting up, and my need for instant gratitude was always bigger than my foresight. I'd say, 'Yes', and 'Of course,' and 'Amn't I the lovely fella?' And then I'd let people down because I couldn't be in three places at the same time. And I'd feel as miserable as an empty bag of crisps for getting myself into this kind of tangle. And I always put it down to immaturity. But some would say it was just bad manners.

In the eighties, there were no mobile phones, so arrangements had to be made in advance and it was very important that both parties held up their end of the bargain. Otherwise, someone was going to be left waiting – someone was going to be annoyed. But that was part and parcel of the game in the casino of love. You had to be prepared to lose as well as win. And you couldn't just phone and say, 'I'm running late.' Phones back then were attached to the wall or sitting on the lovely mahogany phone seat in the hall. And worse still, they were liable to be answered by someone's mother. Ringing your lovely girlfriend and getting her mother was not in the contract. If you were lucky, she wouldn't be a cantankerous rip.

'Who's this?'

'What do ya want?'

'She's not here!'

'That girl has exams!'

'That girl is in her room!'

'That girl has an awful rash on her elbow!'

Or even worse, you could get the slightly inappropriate mother: 'Well, hello there. So you're the lovely young man I see at Mass every once in a while, with your lovely big thighs and that auld puss you do put on ya coming down from Communion. Oh, you are as virile as a young short-horn bull out on after-grass. I'll get Mary in a minute. But do you talk at all, or are you just for cuddlin'?'

Part of the fun of relationships back in the day was the 'Sure, I might see you Thursday. I might be going such a place ...' and not exactly making ... exact plans. But you could daydream till the cows came home about 'what if ...' and 'what if I didn't?' If we wanted everything to be definite, we'd make an appointment with the doctor or the dentist. The best part of love for

me was the 'not knowing'. And in that regard my girlfriends were never disappointed – the poor lasses never
knew whether I was going to turn up or not.

I had nothing against them ... any of them ... it *was*
me. I had nothing going for me except big thighs and big
hands. I couldn't talk to them right. I couldn't say what
I wanted to say. I'd be walking my lovely girlfriend back
to the car of a moonlit night with her sparkling eyes and
that expectant look on her face and I'd get all thoughtful and and romantic and sincere. I'd go into the good
parlour of my mind for nice words. Blow off the dust of
an auld sonnet. Believe me, it doesn't work!

I was so ill-equipped to make small talk. And yet,
some of the thickest bollixes I knew seemed to get away
with whatever they were whispering about when I'd see
them at a disco in Mohill or Ballinamore, with the woman
rubbing against them like a cow's tail and ... smoochy,
smoochy all the way ... And then, mutter, mutter into her
ear ... and she'd swoon and melt all over him like a knob
of butter on a turnip. Where did all that come from?
Every time I opened my mouth in those circumstances,
sirens went off in my head. Dhaaaaaahhhh ... Red Alert!
Red Alert! Wrong choice of words: delete! Delete! But
you can't delete, you can't un-say, 'If a picture paints a
thousand words, then why can't I paint you ...?' You

can't go all Kojak and quoting poetry, especially if it's said randomly … thrown in, in the middle of a conversation about normal things. My idea of romance and my ability to see it through were oceans apart. And what did I expect? There was no romance in our house.

If I rang a girlfriend from our phone at home, the Auld Lad would barge in with his big innocent face. 'Will you be on that phone long? I have to call the AI man.'

The only romance taken seriously in our house was with the animals! Cows looking for the bull was more important than the passionate musings of a 21-year-old. And so, what if I had made a date with three different girlfriends and failed to turn up for any of them? At least they were saved the torture of having to listen to my misplaced romantic dribble.

I took a sip of the pint. Then a gulp. I was going to drink it, and then I'd drink another. This was the first time I had turned to alcohol instead of dealing with my problems. And I knew it wasn't a solution, but I was now weak as well as dishonest. It was one of those moments when you know you're starting to slide, but instead of grasping onto something quickly, you take away your hands altogether and let yourself go.

My uncle Michael double-dated in the early '50's. He had arranged to meet a girl at Kilbrackan bridge near Carrigallen one night, and another girl that he fancied the next night. But he got the nights mixed up, and they both turned up the same night. Michael hid in the bushes – he couldn't face the music. The two women fell out when they realised they were both waiting to meet the same man. My uncle fairly enjoyed that! The only thing was – that wasn't the end of the story. Fast forward to 2011 – almost 60 years later – these same two ladies end up in the same nursing home and start to fight again, over that same night. Had to be sundered by staff in the day room of Laurel Lodge nursing home, in Longford. They were well in their eighties and still hurting. Never underestimate the pain of rejection.

My housemates used to slag me – say I was some man to have three girlfriends. And, of course, I didn't have three girlfriends. If I was any kind of man, I'd have one girlfriend and turn up to meet her and talk to her and treat her right. Three or more at one time … is just silly. Besides, it would only lead to jealousy and violent conduct in nursing homes! And, anyway, I didn't need a girlfriend because I had a new companion. Someone who wouldn't get jealous or cold, or ask, 'What ya thinking?' My new friend would always be there for me, and after a timid start to our relationship, we were now going steady!

My new friend was DRINK.

There wasn't a problem that couldn't be solved by having a pint. Horse them into ya and you'll never have a problem again. No woman problems, no work problems – no problems with your Auld Lad. Just open up your broad and welcoming shoulders and get the pints down as quickly as you can. And numbers are important. It's important to count how many pints you have before you do anything. Eight pints before your first piddle – and five between, after that! Anything under ten doesn't count. Eleven or twelve is a quiet drink. Fifteen is a good session and over twenty is a heavy enough auld night. I applied myself to my new favourite pastime – always up for a pint. I'd even forego food for pints. I could not eat for at least a day if there were enough pints. And it had to be pints – I had learned my lesson with whiskey.

One bank holiday weekend, I went into Carrigallen early and got well steamed. Asked loads of people back to our house for a party. Our house – in Drumshangore, with the Auld Pair asleep in the room at the end of the corridor. What was I thinking? My little sister tried in vain to get me to rethink my idea, but no, I was having a party and that was it. When I got home, there was a traffic jam around the house: I had asked every gobshite from Carrigallen and beyond to come back. And they came in their droves, piled in on the back street. It was like the bumper cars at Bundoran. I went into the house and opened up the good sideboard where the whiskey was kept for the visitors. There were bottles there from the Civil War. Sips and nips of whiskey handed out to dry auld shites of far-out relations and not one of them able to drink properly. Not like the newest alcoholic on the block. I got my hands on five naggins of Paddy. 'WHISKEY … and leave the bottle,' I said in my best American accent. And I opened the bottle and decided I wasn't sharing. I don't remember much after that.

Gene O'Kelly told me years later that I conked out, and that when he and my brother, Kevin, tried to carry me to the bedroom, I woke up and made a swing at my brother and said, 'Lucky I missed ya!' I had never thrown a punch at anyone before or since – lucky is right.

These bloody internationals

The plane took off. We were going to London to play football. We left on Saturday, the 30th of May 1987. The game was the next day. Only the second time that Leitrim had gone to London to play London. The first time was in 1982. These were like visits to the moon. I was lucky to be playing – lining out at midfield with Micky Quinn. 'I suppose yez could make history,' the Auld Lad remarked. 'If yez get bet.' A great boost to a fella's confidence. But, as always, he was right. There was a chance that we could get beaten, and that would be a disaster. Unwanted history makers – the first Connaught team to lose in London.

I was still only twenty-two, but my lofty dreams of sporting achievement were a thing of the past. I was now a realist like my father. And yet still playing football with Leitrim and still getting a game. But now 'CRAIC' was my priority, and everything else could take a back seat. Football, work, the new milking parlour, Mass – they were all fillers now. Now, I was up for divilment of all kinds – drinking pints and not giving a fuck about anything. My mother and father hadn't a clue what I was up to – and a good job! I was living life with such abandonment – well, I thought I was, anyway. Or maybe I was just like everyone else at the time – trying to make the most of a country that was gasping for breath. The young people were fleeing. The Church had mice and all roads led to the pub. At the weekends it was 90 per cent craic and 10 per cent guilt – for what we were doing to our parents. During the week it was all guilt and football training because we couldn't afford pints.

It was around this time I suffered a spate of invitations to graduation ceremonies – young women thinking I would be good company for their big day. That this once quiet-as-a-Zanussi-washing-machine lump of a young fella had come out of himself, and that he was now talking and sometimes making funny comments and was … almost normal. Of course, I wasn't near normal and college graduations were only a reminder to me of what I had left behind when I was fifteen. When I was so sure that I didn't want to stay at school. When I was so convinced that taking the first job that came my way was the way forward – the perfect career choice – that I was going to be so preoccupied with being great that I wouldn't notice the fact that everyone else had matured and was a damn sight further on than me.

The job in Dublin was mind-numbing. We were called cabinet makers because we were making cabinets. But all the cabinets were the same – mostly for the new general hospital in Cavan. Ash veneer cabinets everywhere. It was sickening and the money wasn't great either. But Mr Foley and his son were genuinely nice people, and I was hanging on because I hadn't bothered looking for a job anywhere else. Dublin was great. The summer had arrived, and when the sun came out, I rode my bike to work. And beautiful women blossomed all over the streets. I was often accused of being blind the way I rode my bike – bumping into cars and pedestrians. But I wasn't blind. I could see the slinky tops and the tanned legs of these beautiful girls – was there anything else to look out for? By the time I arrived at work, I'd be a flush of horniness and frustration. I needed lessons on how to get a woman ... and what to do with her when I had her. I was reluctant to ask others what they got up to in the small hours when they went off with their girlfriends or someone else's girlfriend. None of mine ever came with a manual, so I didn't really know.

There was a young country lad working with me in Dublin. Danny Grattan. Danny was younger than me, but he fairly talked the talk when it came to women. Oh, such a one was lovely … and 'I'd love to get her outside!', and 'If I had her outside!' And he was forever going on about getting these women outside. And Paddy Hayes eventually asked him one day: 'And, Danny, what would you do with her if you got her outside?' Danny was quick to reply. 'I'd fucking kiss the shite out of her!'

In 1987 we were in the middle of the great 'condom crisis'. I didn't know what a condom was at the time or how they worked – all I knew was that everyone wanted them. And they were probably required if you were going to go round kissing the shite out of women. It was against the law to sell them or distribute them at the time. All forms of contraception, apart from 'keep it in your trousers', were banned in Ireland. But not in Northern Ireland or London, where we were going to play our game.

The only other place you could get condoms in the '80s was in Arvagh – a small town a few miles from Carrigallen. Jim Williamson was the chemist there. Jim had broader vision than most … and most thought that Jim Williamson was mad. But he wasn't mad. He was informed – and he had opinions. Not like the rest of us. Jim held counsel on every topic, except football and foolish love. He loved animals and wildlife and slow horses. He questioned everything, including the Church and the price of fags. He believed in ghosts and fairies and making money. And he didn't agree with the laws banning the sale of contraceptives. So he purchased consignments of 'rubber jonnies' from the North and sold them under the counter. No winking or nodding – just ask you straight out, 'Do you want a half dozen of these fellas?' And Jim kept manners on the population, better than most.

The likes of me and a small minority of the Leitrim football team were not in the loop when it came to togging out in condoms – pure and as innocent as a small hen. And so, after our narrow win in London on the 31st of May 1987, we weren't the ones firing pound coins into the condom machine every time we went into the men's toilet. I didn't see the practicality of having condoms available in the lavatories of London pubs. But my randy teammates were grinning from ear to ear knowing they were laden down with extreme protection. Later that night, when we got thrown out of the pub, four of the same lads were wrestling in the middle of the street over sandwiches – and got arrested and brought off to a police station and asked to remove everything from their pockets. They timidly removed enough rubber to cover a small silage pit at home. The arresting officers falling around the place laughing at the sheer optimism of these Irish boys, as the rest of us gathered outside shouting, 'We want justice for the Leitrim Four'. The incident never got leaked to the press – the *Leitrim Observer* too caught up in the traffic light saga. Leitrim was under threat at the time – proposals afoot to install a traffic light in the county. They just didn't know where to put it.

Some footballers in the seventies and eighties could get away with excessive drinking, while still playing football at a high level. I was different. Even without drinking I wasn't able to play at a high level. And with pints now playing a big part in my world, my days were numbered. I lost my place for the next championship game to an up-and-coming Paul Kiernan from Ballinamore. Paul was as laid back as he was talented, and to rub salt into my wounds, five minutes before we ran out onto the field for the next game, I was asked to give Paul my boots, as his were in tatters.

When we got home from the London game on the bank holiday Monday, myself and a few of the lads went for pints. I was also off work the following day, and so I continued drinking. Between that and the disappointment over how I had played, I failed to show up for work on the Wednesday. On Thursday morning

I was met by Mr Foley, and he smiled and said, 'Oh, Seamus, Liam Brady always says the same thing – these bloody internationals are the worst!' And he laughed ... but I didn't. That was the first time I had missed work because of alcohol, and I was disappointed. If I could only remember how much craic I'd had.

That was the longest time I'd spent not working ... in my life. Five days in a row – my mother and father would have been ashamed. Ever since we could stand, we were encouraged to help out, to do our bit – to work. There was no time off or holidays in our house. I tried my case with the Auld Lad over bank holidays, but no, bank holidays were for people who worked in the bank. I thought surely church holidays. But no – that was a day that the Church gave us to catch up on work. So, what about summer holidays? No, never. I did have one vague recollection of being in Bundoran one summer, but my mother now tells me that we were just visiting people who were on their own holidays – that we were not actually on holidays ourselves ... and anyway, we didn't stay long.

With the result, I've always found it hard to do nothing, and yet I'm not overly fond of work. Football had been a great filler, until I got carried away by it. The glamour and the glory of it – the glamour and the glory that never came my way. I had promised much, but ultimately, I had shit on the eggs. The weekend after London and still feeling sorry for myself, I met Kevin Mitchell after Mass. Kevin was Pat's younger brother – younger than me – not a footballer or an athlete, but he said he was going for a run later that day and that he was hoping to do the Dublin City Marathon. I said I'd tag along. I arranged to meet him at the bottom of our lane. He was a gangly sort, only twenty at the time; no real shape or make to him – just a young lad out for a run. We didn't talk much – just ran – the road was familiar, as was the sound of my heavy feet. The sound of leaving football behind.

On my knees

My knees were weak. And not from being in love. Ever since I was a boy, my knees were the boys to let me down. If it wasn't one of them, it was the other. At first, Dr Farrelly told me it was growing pains – that I was too big too soon. But even when I was finished growing, my knees still gave me trouble. When I was in New York and able to lift the gable end of Manhattan with my big thighs – it was my arthritic knees that started to crumble. I think that's what's going to get me in the end. The knees. I wouldn't mind if the problem was something sexy, like cruciate ligament. But, no – just two bad knees. They'd be grand for a while and then – plop – sit down on me and I wouldn't be able to walk for days. When I was twelve, I remember reversing up the steps at Drumeela church, because my knees were at me. Running on the road was not recommended for anyone standing 6 foot 2 and weighing in or around the 16 stone mark.

'Where are you going with them knees?' my mother asked.

'He's trying to find the quickest way into the hospital,' my father said.

Well, they were never going to say, 'That's a great idea … hope you enjoy your run.'

I was now running regularly with Kevin Mitchell – if you could call my stride regular! The Mitchells lived on the edge of Newtowngore village. At the time it was a lively centre of warmth and enthusiasm – a warm house – an even warmer welcome. Sheila and Danny Mitchell and their three sons, Pat, Kevin, and John, had an open house and there was always someone calling – always cups of tea and whatever we young ones were up to got sifted through and blessed. Danny Mitchell was a big gruff man, a blacksmith by trade who worked in McCartin's Engineering – the only one there to use size six welding rods regardless of what job he was at. 'Never use a hammer when you have a sledge lying there beside ya.' That was Danny's motto. As straight and as straightforward as you could find. He was an older man when he married Sheila and he played 'the wise old man' well. But beneath his tough exterior, there was a pair of dancing eyes, lapping up the frivolity of his three young sons and their friends. Sheila was a fairy godmother of a woman – as light and polite – dancing attendance on all who entered her domain. Positivity thrown around as if it were plentiful as the biscuits and buns, the sweet cake and dainty cups. Not something I was accustomed to. I often felt like bottling what went on in the Mitchells' home – the sweet cake, the good wishes and the kind remarks.

Across the road from the Mitchell house was Richardson's sawmill. An expansive yard of sheds and piles and piles of Sitka spruce. Yet another thriving business in Newtowngore. Danny had an agreement with the Richardsons to dispose of their offcuts. In his spare time, he'd take his wheelbarrow and go across and cut these offcuts to size and stack them on the wheelbarrow and wheel them back to his blacksmith's shed where they were stored until ready to burn. It was such a familiar sight to see Danny crossing the road with his wheelbarrow stacked to twice its capacity and wavering in the sight of oncoming traffic. When he retired from the Engineering, he became a full-time gatherer of firewood. The routine and the meticulous nature in which he carried it out was now a substitute for something lost – a forgotten time and the enchantment that once filled his home.

I went for lots of runs with Kevin, but I also liked the solitude of running alone. I always timed my escape when the Auld Lad was away or preoccupied in some way. His look of disappointment at my running for no reason was hard to swallow. He could see the sense in football and competitive sport. But going out jogging or walking or riding a bike aimlessly and all that had to be done around the house: 'It's the pure sign of an eejit,' he'd say. And he was sure he was right. 'Eejit' was a popular word in our house growing up. My parents didn't curse or swear, so we were just called eejits at every turn. They word 'eejit' is derived from the more formal admonishment 'idiot', meaning someone of lesser intelligence. Of course, our 'eejit' was a much looser term and bandied about with gusto. A pure eejit – a half-eejit – a buck-eejit – a horrid eejit – a thunderous eejit. And if there was any doubting the particular type, we'd be asked, 'What kind of an eejit are ya?' A rhetorical question that always hit the sweet spot.

I'd tog out in the bedroom of the new house. Still in a room with my brother – his side tidy and respectable – my side untidy and irresponsible. A few half-hearted stretches and I was off out the door and down the lane. At the end of the lane, I turned right where the milk lorry turned every morning. The lovely old piers and the ornate gates taken down and the lane widened to make way for oncoming changes. I headed towards

Corrawallen, past McCaffery's gate where McCaffery dug up the road to slow down the young pups, Patterson and Woods, on their motorbikes. On by Tom Mimna's lane and the tidiness of the place struck me. You could eat your dinner off Tom Mimna's front street. The small garden holding its breath in the fear it might fart a weed. I jogged on up the hill where I could see Drumshangore Bog to my right and Toome Lane coming into view. And then Hugh Murray's house and Mrs Woods's lovely old cottage and the gardens and derelict walls to McCabe's – the crab apples in good supply this year. It was August and the hedges and trees whispered hope as I climbed the slight incline towards Hyland's shop. Then, as the landscape began to disappear and the chambers of my most inward thoughts took over, I began to dally.

Where was I going in my life? A melting river of dreams and longings. As a boy, I wanted to save the world. To help the weary – to give the men a hand making hay – and give rest to women who did men's work. Women like my mother – lifting and carrying and barely carrying on. When I was a boy, I had no needs of my own. I only wanted enough to eat and a warm bed to sleep in. I wanted to rock babies to sleep and soothe the groans of our calving cows – to jam my finger in the fountain of blood coming from the half-cut horns and to rub the new-born calf with hay until it spluttered and coughed and came to life – like my father did. I wanted to race ahead of the herd and stand in gateways and gaps in hedges – to make standing in gaps my art. I had so many good intentions ... but I wasn't meant for this. The land and the livestock and our parents' and neighbours' plight was not my fight – it was my brother's. I needed to find my own fight and I needed to find it soon. Was it my father's fault or where I was born, or how much I was inclined to be distracted? Was that why I couldn't see what was in front of me? I wanted to know what was inside of me ... but the road came back to meet me.

I was now running through the heart of Drumreilly, the byroads there, surrounded by the smallest of fields – fields not tampered with or reclaimed, but left alone. There's a lot to be said for leaving things as they were. But I couldn't stay the same; that's not the way I was made. What use would I be to anything if I stayed as I was now? Giving a half-hearted handshake to everything and yet gripping nothing tight.

I ran almost twelve miles that day, my daydreams running away with me. I finally came to a halt gasping for air and perspective. The next day I couldn't get out of bed. It was the knees – and the running for no reason.

I didn't do much road running after that. I tried to start again the following year. I was going to run the Dublin City Marathon in memory of my friend Kevin Mitchell, who died in a road accident on the 4th of July 1988 – but the knees wouldn't let me remember him. I hid his death deep in the underbelly of my consciousness, until one night with the help of alcohol and an inquisitive friend, I let it all out. Cried like a child – me – that has such a great capacity to not cry.

I had lost a friend, but with that, I also lost my haven for the lost – Mitchell's hub in Newtowngore. It was no longer the centre of fun and positivity because a thing called sadness now hung outside their door ... and we stopped calling. The planning and scheming, the dainty cups of tea and the sweet cake, that was all redundant now. Like we were all being made pay for the freak tragedy that took our friend. It's hard to make up with God after that. And Danny Mitchell's sternness, once wrestled away by the constant yelps of youthful delight, had now a permanent hold on him. For the rest of his long life, he wheeled his barrowfuls of firewood across the road, without ever diverting his gaze. Sheila used what love she had left on Danny and Pat and John and always tried her best to be as ignited and as bright as a broken-hearted mother could be.

I hate death and what it fails to bring out in me. It brings out the best in some – some are so quick to respond – to help – to just be around. I haven't those qualities, I've built barriers. Forged them through years of not dealing with death and the finality of not seeing our loved ones anymore. And I've made these barriers strong and secure. I have no time for tap-dancing around death – the dainty cups of tea and the 'Sorry for your troubles'. It's a selfish attitude, I know – one that I'm not proud of – but one that sees me through … for now. Some of my friends have been taken. Some quickly and some have been taken slow. I'm just not clear on why.

The house is sleeping

The number of residents in our half a house for three on Richmond Road had risen to five. We decided to move – not far – to Mabel Street, even closer to Croke Park. It was an entire house – not a very big one – for five inhabitants. But the extra lodgers kept coming. Soon there were more than five – more and more bodies on the floor, more and more dirty socks in the windows, more dirty dishes in the sink and less space in the fridge!

And although I was the original tenant – once the sole occupant of that first bedsit on the North Circular Road – Donie McLoughlin had now taken over as head of the expanded household. Not by choice, but because none of the rest of us were mature enough to deal with rent and when the bins had to be filled and taken out. And he was the tallest. And he was domesticated – well, certainly in our eyes. And he could use an iron. Donie could unfold the ironing board like a magician and wrestle the hot iron into a zigzag forward motion,

causing the removal of creases from his shirt. The rest
of us used the laws of gravity. And he could cook –
his demonstration of how to cook an entire dinner of
spuds and lamb cutlets while positioned on a stool in
the middle of our kitchen has stayed with me a lifetime.
Although the kitchen was quite small, only a man with
arms twice the length of his body could manage a feat
like that. He was a good footballer too and well used
to minding the house for Fenagh and Leitrim football
teams. Donie and Thomas Quinn were cornerbacks
on the Leitrim Senior team when I played at full back.
They were both well fed up with minding me on the
football field and now Donie got to mind me during
the week as well. He knew my shortcomings and my
bouts of laziness. He was the only one who tidied up
after me – or anyone else. That was about to change.
He called us all together one Wednesday evening and
gave us a talk on personal hygiene and tidying up after
ourselves and not eating his lamb cutlets or his margarine. I would never eat another man's margarine, no
matter how desperate I was. But we thought he was
joking about the tidying; we all thought that he'd do
like our mothers – that he'd just get fed up with the
mess and go back to tidying up and minding us. But
no, that was it. He was calling time on his caring career.

As cold and as callous an act as you could imagine and the big, long arms of him!

In the early hours of a mild Monday morning – after a weekend of rampant sex and general untidiness – I watched a small mouse on the bedroom floor. He was tip-toeing his way to a piece of stale bread left beside a bedside locker. The bread was a full slice of bread, buttered and whole, and only 14 days old. It wasn't the mouse's first appointment of the night. He had already left his footprints in the jam and the margarine which lay open on the sitting room table. Indeed, this mouse might have considered this room unsuitable for further foraging if he had been around earlier, when we were hit by a furious gust of toxic fumes that swirled and galed through the lower regions of the congested space. My muttered disgust not heard among the snores and groans of the hefty human inhabitants. A tiny mouse caught in that whirlwind could easily end up with his paws aloft in the dead-mouse position.

But the mouse had survived and was nibbling away, with the rest of the house still sleeping. I counted in my head how many men lay dreaming. One, two, three, four, five … and Donie and me … and Brendan Conway – eight. Oh, and Thomas Lynch – he had just arrived. Nine … in a house for five. The paint was peeling and the floorboards lifting, the stairs were creaking and the air was humming. The house encapsulating the youth of the day. Sleeping and snoring and smacking parched gums. It could have easily been mistaken for an infirmary, where tired bodies hung from shared beds and makeshift sleeping bags. Only enough clean clothes and pure thoughts to last till Thursday. Empty beer cans lay lingering and an ashtray smouldering. Someone had left their transistor on – turned as low as it could go – only in the quiet of the Drumcondra night could it be heard. Fats Domino finding himself on Blueberry Hill again. Outside, someone was shouting 'Up the Ra' ... but no one seemed to care whether the Ra was up or down.

I longed for the comforts of home – if I could remember any of the comforts of home. We grew up in a cold house with two hot water bottles and a paraffin heater between six. We warmed our pyjamas by the chimney breast upstairs and shivered our way through our prayers. We didn't even have mice – it was too cold. But every now and again, if we were really sick and had to stay home from school, we'd be sent to bed during the day with a whole hot water bottle to ourselves. Mammy would make tea and toast. We only had toast when someone was sick. The Auld Lad didn't agree with burning good bread. The smell of toast would make its way upstairs and the tea would follow – hot and full of love. Mammy wouldn't have time to sit, but she'd make the bed while you were in it. That was the greatest thing I knew. Layer by layer, she'd shroud us in comfort – shake out the sheets above our head and so gently they would fall. Then a blanket and another, and at the end, she'd tuck them in, and our cocooning was complete – as snug and as warm in body and spirit as either of us dared to mention. My mother was full of the complexities of any woman, plus another few of her own. She took on so much, she was always cautious of letting slip precious moments like these.

I wouldn't want to patronise the women of that time, least of all my mother, but she had some job on her hands. With us – with me. But she always looked to the road ahead – she never had time to ponder. In some ways, that suited her style. Mammy was a fighter, but also a woman who was capable of extreme acts of generosity and kindness. Making me tea and toast and tucking the worn thin blankets under my skin was one of them. The memory that comforts me most. But there was none of that from when I got big. Not at home, and certainly not in Mabel Street. Maybe Dublin wasn't what I needed.

I once sat by Portobello House at the Grand Canal, after I arrived in Dublin. It was the height of summer,

and the Dublin weather was so much better than ours.
I got Patrick Kavanagh's point about not making hay. It
was great hay weather, and yet here I was sitting looking
into the water. There had been young ones jumping in ...
but they had drifted off into the evening. Of course, I
wasn't alone, but I felt alone – in a good way – finding
it hard to believe that there was such beauty in the city.
The last of the sun's heat kept me warm and the stillness
of the canal held me. Our rivers at home were always
racing – never still – never calm. And I was never calm.
Oh, I seemed quiet and thoughtful, but I was never
really calm. But I was that evening by the canal. One
of those moments you'd like to put in a jar and put the
lid on – like when my mother tucked me in. I'll always
cherish that Dublin: in the tail end of the evening when
everyone's gone home. But that's not how I felt now.

It was now 5.30 a.m. I still wasn't sleeping. Then
the first alarm of the morning went ping. A gentle watch
alarm – newfangled at the time and on time. But the
alarm was not the nuisance here. It was the clunk of
Brendan Conway's feet, thrown out on the bedroom
floor like railway sleepers. Unaware of what such an
early thud could do to sleeping dolls, he took in to
tramp and groan and yawn and fart – as heavy and as
loud as an ass and cart. And slurping milk from a carton

and finding keys and then in the big loud Cloone voice, 'Is anyone awake?' And all in turn would let Brendan know that 'We are now, ya bollix'.

I was the guts of two years in Dublin. And like New York, I love it still. But still, it wasn't fulfilling any dreams. The craic was always great, but this constant living on top of each other was getting on my nerves. And everyone was great, and we never fought or talked behind each other's backs – but I wasn't cut out for communal living. I could create my own mess, my own smells. I didn't need seven hairy arses to make my life exciting, I didn't need to be reminded to pay the rent or put out the bins. I could forget to do that by myself. And again, I thought of moving home. Not for the comfort of home, but the stability of home. I didn't know it yet, but I was one of those boring auld shites who didn't want to go anywhere – who was happy enough to live where I was born.

There's a lot made of travelling, like there's a lot made of education, and most are better off because of both – but some are not. Some like their home patch where they don't have to ask for direction or instruction. Some don't need the hassle of finding out.

I made contact with my old boss, Tommy Reilly. He had every right to tell me to go take a running jump for myself, but he didn't. He was expanding and looking for help. He gave me the start. I was sad to say goodbye to Mr Foley and his son at Irish Woodworking Ltd, and they said they were sad that I was moving on. But I've never had a problem moving on. Once the page is written, there's no point lingering – there's always a blank page somewhere else. Maybe that page was somewhere nearer home.

Parlour games

I always shared a room with my brother – shared a bed
for long enough. But even when we built the new bungalow, with all four bedrooms, someone had to share.
So there was one for my parents; one each for the girls;
and me and Kevin got the last one – to share. Two single
beds. His side of the room and my side. You'd know
who slept where if you saw it. The only time I ever saw
Kevin in bed was when I'd stay out late – he'd be there
sleeping away when I got home. And when I'd wake
up, he'd be gone. He was always up before me. It was
a great comfort knowing that he was up and had the
universe ticking over before I put my feet to the floor.

Weekday mornings started with a start. 'Are you
getting up?' my mother would repeat. The sound of the
radio in the kitchen: *Morning Ireland* and *What the
Papers Say* – news being fired out in all directions. My
father and my mother, in and out of the house, disturbing everyone, finishing off 'doing the things'. Rubbin' it

in that I had it handy. My brother up since six, cows milked and strigged and carried back out to the field; the milking machine sundered and washed and put back together again; calves fed and nuts brought to the four corners of the earth – all while I was picking fluff out of my bellybutton.

I had a five-minute drive in the car to my work – five and a half if there was traffic. The radio on to fill the void. To the gate and nothing coming. To the cross – look both ways. Harte's-of-the-bridge and keep her going; past the mart and on I go. The fingerboard then, and all is with me – through the town without a care. Most mornings I closed out the world and searched for a reason to carry on. Most days I faked my signature on a job well done. If this was what I wanted, I hadn't set the bar too high. I was open to persuasion. The vultures looking down on my innocence and thinking: *We'll miss you when you're gone.*

Wakening at the weekend was a very different thing altogether. No Mammy shouting. No radio bluffing. The sound of everyone gone – the sound of missing out. No sound. It can be a nice sound … or an unnerving one. There's always a great chance that our relevance will be questioned if there's no sound. In 1988, the low dull sound of men contemplating came through my window.

My father and my brother were wondering about building a new milking parlour at the end of the existing byre, with a new dairy somewhere near. They were roughly stepping out the foundation with short steps and long – a farmer's step, long or short, is a yard or thereabouts. Teamwork in very short supply. Neither accepting nor suggesting. Just lots of wondering. A fear to commit – in case it might turn into a bucket with a hole. They were hard watched when they were locking horns over a new project. I wasn't an expert, but I was a godsend in these situations. They needed a doer – someone who didn't care as much as them. And in me they had their man. The three of us worked well together. Neither of them knew what they wanted, but at least they knew what they didn't want, and I was fairly good at finding the handiest way round most chores. I replaced their rival steps with a measuring tape, and we set to work, marking with chalk powder as we went. If they wanted more space, I would give them more space. If we needed to move something, we moved it. Their only annoyance was its simplicity. After all their clutching to half-thought-out ideas, they relaxed their thinking and common sense did prevail. Then it was time for tea.

My mother was slow to broach the subject of what was going on. The dread of another marathon of a building match. The scars had barely healed from the building of the dwelling house. That house had caused more sulks and breakdowns and unfinished tea. You couldn't take tea with some of what went on at the building of the bungalow. And my father wasn't getting any younger and did we really need a milking parlour? The questions outweighed the answers. The answers – hanging by a thread. But the tea was poured, and the debate was thrown out on the table, and we all had our say – tempers flickering and there was sarcasm coming from every corner. And yet this was as happy as we got. The gates of communication swung open for the briefest of moments, and then it was time for me to go. Hanging around at our breakfast table will only get you a job. I didn't mind sorting out the plans or the approach, but I wasn't going to be there for the hard work. I'd only be in the way.

Stuck for places to go, I went to the football pitch. I had a few balls in the car and my gear, and I did what was so regular and natural a few years before. I went for a kick around. But this Saturday, I really went to the park to avoid work. My boots were dirty, and my socks were crispy. The pleasure of clean gear denied by neglect. Football slipping down the ladder of priorities. The ladder of dreams, all but disabled. I was cruising at an altitude of low expectations.

I togged out in the dressing rooms and walked past the town goals and out onto the pitch. I never walked that walk before. Anytime I went there, I ran – I raced – with fire in my belly. My head and my heart filled with love for the game. The game that used to make me shiver with excitement. Used to make me weak at the knees. Now, my knees were in constant pain, and I had lost my desire. I was tired of mediocrity – tired of having the odd middlin' game. Just tired of my limitations.

I was suddenly aware of someone watching – a tall man standing at the town goals as I was lazily kicking balls up the other end. Who was this nosy hoor snooping? I kicked a ball in his direction, and he came towards me. He had the gait of a farmer – wellingtons a go-go as he made a swing at the rolling ball. I had seen that ungainly frame before. It was Patsy Foy.

Patsy Foy was a sub on the 1980 Junior team. I was fifteen then – he was thirty. He never got a game. He wasn't a footballer. Just a young man who wanted a bit of company. He wasn't a drinker either and there's not a lot else to do in rural areas if you don't drink or play football. Patsy was a through-other sort: baling twine his main sponsor – he used it for everything. He was the butt of a few smart jibes in his time, but they said Patsy was a smart enough sort of fool. He did Latin and

Greek for his Leaving Cert in Moyne in 1967 – a very bright man, who chose farming as his companion, and the two of them danced and wrestled and acted the goat till the day he died.

'Hello there, young man,' he casually uttered – a nonchalant approach to a county man. 'A Mr O'Rourke, I believe. Seamus, I think …?'

I said it was.

'I remember you from the Junior final. I could see great promise. You must have been very young back then?'

'Fifteen,' I said, compounding his admiration.

'A prodigy, I suppose they'd call you. At the time, mind you, if you had followed the trajectory you were on, you'd be an All-Star by now. Or off playing this Aussie Rules that they seem to admire so much.'

I smiled and said, 'Oh now …' Half accepting the compliment – half wondering was it a compliment at all.

'It doesn't really take you anywhere, does it?'

He left that remark sitting there for a moment. I was now aware that Patsy Foy was not the fool that I and many others had taken him for. This was the first time I had ever talked to the man.

'How do you mean?' I said.

'If you have a sharp sickle, you must go where there's wheat …' And he left that one sitting there too. 'We were all young. We all had our promise. But it's not what you do with the promise. It's mostly what you do with the disappointment it leaves behind. You're not going to be an All-Star, you probably know that, but you could be something else. I often thought of trying for the bank, but it wouldn't suit me – and I mightn't suit it. But you never know when a bird might alight, or a frog might jump up. I'm out in Miltron trying to encourage cattle to eat less grass – that's not working at the moment. I wish you well. I always wondered how you'd get on in the bright lights. And I saw your car. Keep her lit, if that's what you're into.'

He turned to look at McGarahan's Hill. 'It's no fun being a hill in Leitrim, is it?'

And then he walked away as carelessly as he had walked in. I wanted to call after him ... to say something profound ... but he had taken most of the air with him, and I was left alone to sift through the embers of what he had said. I had never allowed for not being good enough. I felt as lonely and as foolish as if I had piddled in my pants.

I had been in love with Gaelic football since I was seven, and now Gaelic football was seeing someone else. I was angry and annoyed, but mostly, I was stranded. Like in the middle of an empty dancefloor, after asking a beautiful girl out to dance and she had said, 'Not tonight, pet. Not tonight.'

I was in my home football pitch, I was asking Gaelic football, 'Will you please dance with me, because I don't know what I'm going to do if you don't? Please ... please, give me one more chance.'

The netting behind the far goals whistled in the breeze and there was a clanking sound as the pulley wheels touched the stanchions. I used to love that eerie sound.

Just the one

I locked up at work on Tuesday evening. I was supposed to be going to county training, but I didn't feel like it. I had not felt like it many times before, but mostly went … and I always felt the better of my decision. There's something heroic about being 'not much good' at something, yet giving it your all. But heroism can suddenly turn into stupidity, and no one wants that. As I started my car, I was thinking of excuses – which one? I had so many. I was past the point of picking a good one. I was more worried about how I'd spend my evening. The building of the new milking parlour was in full swing. I was sure to be dragged into that after dinner. And I suppose chops again for dinner. I was getting sick of chops. There were always chops and gravy and spuds and carrots and cabbage – like my mother was using a photocopier to dish up culinary delights. She was better than that, but who was going to say it? My father was the head of the family, but as long as there was cabbage, he was happy.

As I drove the short distance from Kivvy into Carrigallen, a clarity came over me. I had never noticed my hometown like this before. Yes, I went there on weekend nights – drank lots and enjoyed the substantial madness attached to the place. But what happened there during the day or early evening was beyond me. I noticed Dougie Stewart and Terry Murray coming out of the hotel and heading into McGuckian's. My car slowed down and stopped. It was an involuntary action. My heart did a little shuffle and there was a sudden change of beat. I clipped my measuring tape onto my belt and went into McGuckian's bar in broad daylight. What the hell was I doing?

I wasn't even a proper drinker. I wasn't one of these lads who had been drinking since they were twelve. I was twenty before I started. And I hadn't been led to it by peer pressure – heading off with a crowd of young ones clutching a crate of beer. I had started drinking with Brian Doyle. Doyle might have had great potential as a footballer, but he was a fairly useless drinker – drunk as anything after six pints. I had no proper apprenticeship done in alcohol consumption – not enough accidents or even near ones; certainly no life-threatening situations like what the genuine drinkers would be going on about. I didn't deserve the right to swan into a lonesome tavern in broad daylight. But I did.

And the daylight disappeared behind me. I was in. It was like I had shrunk in size and crawled into a mouse hole. I was now privy to what the mice were up to when they weren't scurrying across the floor. There were a lot of mice – a few uncomfortable under the stare of a day-person, but most were beyond ridicule. I wasn't sure how to act, but I knew 'excited' wasn't going to cut it. So I fell back on my well-practised calm approach. I almost broke into a half whistle like my father would when in unfamiliar space. Tommy McGuckian was pulling a pint as I walked in. He didn't have to look – he could smell fresh meat. He was a small tidy man. A Monaghan man. A hard-working intense man. A full-time farmer and undertaker as well as a part-time publican. Fed up with standing behind this Formica counter listening to all kinds of half-thought-out nonsense and half-truths. Tommy wasn't cut out for chit-chat – but chit-chat was all a go. And about as relevant, or irrelevant, as the broad array of rosettes for horses and ponies and big bulging cattle that adorned the back bar of this well-stocked public house.

Tommy was astute. He knew a good horse when he saw one … could spot a potential new customer when they came in all empty and full of want. 'Ah Seamus, we don't see you often during the day. What can I get ya?'

'A pint a Guinness, Tommy, please ...' And now, I was having cheese with all the other mice. A new world for me – a new chain – a good heavy chain to hang around my neck.

'Ah hah. And well, Seamus Rourke, and how's all in Drumshangore and Newtowngore? I used to see you in Gorby's drinking minerals. I know your father very well and your mother works here next door in the hotel. She'd do as much as an army a men. Are ya still working at the presses? Is it you that puts in the presses for Tommy Reilly?' Terry Murray piled the questions high. My answers were short and loose and fell carelessly among the fag butts and the ash.

McGuckian's bar was narrow and dark, and a cloud of smoke hung under the low ceiling. Black leatherette seats lined the wall to the left, with round tables and low stools neatly placed. The Cartys were in and John Duffy. Dougie and Terry Murray had already settled. There were others too – all a little put out by the invasion of youth – my youth. They were men of a different world: cattle men, talking of cattle marts and shows. They didn't want the distraction of a gormless passer-by with no interest in man or beast.

It was 5.30 p.m. A quiet time ... uneventful ... before the pints and the half pints. Mostly rum and port, and whiskey and bottles of stout – the drinking man's starter, the drinking man's soup. Some had been in since twelve or one, and some since the latch was lifted at ten o'clock that morning.

These lauded Irish hostelries, with their exaggerated standing in rural life, were just extravagant film sets full of unwanted extras. Men talking sideways across the small tables – filling their day with blanks. Our love affair with these places – our unspoken error of judgement – has for centuries allowed them to nibble away at our toes. We leave the truth of the real world behind to join a world where nothing is real; where nothing has worth, except the art of pretence. These men talked of real things in an environment that wasn't real. They gave passionate speeches about morals and agenda but kept well back from the snarling gaze of reality. Spectators at a peep show. And I was now there with my ticket in my fist.

And of course, my damning review is all in hindsight – the bitter word of someone who couldn't draw away from the mice and the mouse hole. I was never going to bring myself back to a life-size mammal. But at the time, it was exciting and new and hilarious. These places harboured some of the great wits and contradictions of my youth. Never has so much intelligence and imagination been condensed and spewed so generously across my path. Protein for the mind and soul and my inner sanctum of foolishness.

Hughie McGarahan came in then. A man hopping out of his wellingtons with excitement and dying for a drink. He couldn't see right with his glasses, despite pushing them up and down his nose. A glass of Guinness and a brandy and rum. He was only in for one. He had cattle out, but couldn't get his young lads away from the television to help him put them back in. 'They're watching bloody snooker,' and we all knew they had their hands full watching snooker in black and white. Hughie knew me well from the football; he used to do the line. The most corrupt linesman to ever trawl a sideline. One-way traffic – always a Carrigallen ball – as barefaced as you please. A lovely man. At the time he was working with FÁS. A passionate family man who only came into the pub for advice and to give advice and to talk about the gold he had found when he found Bunty, his wife.

Sean Donnelly came in, wondering what I was doing in a pub at that time. Clinging on to me for dear life. Telling me I shouldn't be there – that I was on the slippery slope – but lovely to see me all the same! Told me that I was being badly treated by the county and would

I have a pint. When I said yes, he said, 'I thought you said you were going home?' And that was it for me – I was staying just for spite.

When I did go home, I noticed I had 20 pounds less than I had going in. I lamented the loss of money and time but thought of the jewels I had seen. Jack Nixon shouting high above the crowd – the howls of laughter at McGoohan's missing calves – the low digs flying everywhere and the well-practised story of Joe Clamping and some quare wan holding hands. These men were masters of their craft: storytellers, mimics, jesters of the bar – and I had a ringside seat. As uplifting as a spoon of ginger in your hot milk going to bed.

And, of course, our house had gone to bed when I got home. A note on the table: *Dinner in oven*. And it was. Still warm – chops and spuds and gravy and carrots ... and cabbage. I felt like putting it back. I didn't deserve a dinner after spending the evening in the town. Even wearing my measuring tape didn't make it right. But my mother didn't know that. She probably thought I was working late. *Poor Seamus having to work so late* – and him up to his neck in frivolity in that bloody Carrigallen. I had to eat the dinner; it would have been bad manners not to ... and I was as hungry and as full and as tired – and all at the same time! I tucked in.

In the small hours of the morning, with the kitchen light still on, my mother tip-toed up the long corridor of our L-shaped bungalow. She was in her nightdress, the same nightdress she had worn for donkey's years. My mother refused to pamper herself in any way. She walked into the kitchen. Walked in on her favourite son – sleeping – in his dinner. My face submerged in a gravy ravine, carved from the cabbagey hills and the half-eaten chop hidden under a volcanic spillage of dribble and spuds that nestled under my chin. I was not in a good place. I woke up – snorting and spluttering as I extracted myself from my plate. The look of sadness and surprise on my mother's face. She could be gullible, but for once it was plain to see that I was so fed up with our evening meals.

The chemist

I reversed the old orange Mercedes van as near as I could to the shop door. There was a big clatter on the side of the yoke.

'Woah, woah! Where are you going with the big van?'

Jim Williamson was out in his pyjamas remonstrating about the size of the van and the hour of the morning. 'And I tould that Tommy Reilly too. I tould him when I gave him the go-ahead to put in that bit of a press. I tould him I didn't want him here at all hours. I don't go to bed till four in the morning. I could do with a bit of fucking peace first thing. Who are you? Oh, I know your face … You're the football man. You're in that Drumeela Macra. There's some great actors down there in Drumeela. How come I don't see you on stage?'

It was eventually my turn to speak. 'I'm afraid that wouldn't be my scene,' I said.

'You only think that – a big good-lookin' fella like ya. Pull the hoor of a van away from that door and let the fucking people in and out. Will ya eat a boiled egg?'

'No thanks ...'

And that was my introduction to Jim Willy – the chemist in Arvagh. I didn't know whether to laugh or run away.

Jim was a Dickensian pharmacist. A man in his early forties, but you could add or subtract at least two score years, depending on his state of 'being' at the time. He could be as wise or as childish as you liked, but never indifferent ... except for football. He had no time for young people running around after a ball of wind. Jim was a rally man – car racing and drink and fags and reading thick books. And all in the extreme, till he gave up the drink and became even more extreme about everything else. His newest craze was amateur drama. He had joined the Carrigallen Community Players a couple of years before and was smitten for life.

'I'm not great at the acting, but I can see what it's about. Some of these smart fellas think they know it all, but they know sweet fuck all! Do ya know Peter McNamee?'

I was so bamboozled by the lecture I didn't know whether I did or I didn't. Jim was boiling three eggs. I was bringing in the tools, preparing to put in the press.

'Do ya read?' says he.

'No,' says I.

'And what kind of a bollix are ya? And are you that good at the football that you'll never have to do anything else?'

I smiled … There was no answer to that.

'Do ya run after women itself?'

'I do.'

'Of course ya do. The women love the big lads with the bit of height. Be careful at that auld ridin'. I have rubbers there in packs of three. Don't be stuck. Don't be a bollix. I'm not sure of the price of them. I'm not giving them away and me breaking the law to have them; but buy a go of them and have them in the van or the car in case you fall in love all of a sudden and are going around with a big horn and no protection. The Church doesn't want you to use them, because they only want your sins. That's their line of business. Push you into a corner with a young one and then send down a big erection and sexy music. You'd want some hand-brake to stall on that hill! There'll be war yet with this Church and all the things that went on. Oh, it'll come out yet. You'll see some changes in this country over the next few years. The bastards think they're getting away with it, but there's too big a tear in the bag now. The secrets are spilling out all over the place. Are you sure you won't have an egg?'

Jim's lovely big Alsatian dog, Bruce, had his own horn to contend with, as he sat listening to all the talk about sex and the Church and an acting course in Gormanstown. He was the first house dog that I was aware of and him as big as a suck calf and as mild-mannered as a kitten. Jim loved Bruce and Bruce loved the bits of boiled egg that fell from Jim Willy's spoon. But the eating of the eggs was a marathon in itself – took about three hours – an hour an egg – on account of the shop. The bell of the shop door would ring as Jim was nibbling away, describing to me the similarities between Anton Chekhov and John B. Keane. I had heard of John B. Keane, but not the other one. Then Jim would shoot off to the shop to fill a prescription, argue about politics, or shoehorn the topic of theatre into someone's athlete's foot. Then he'd return. Two and a half eggs down – a spoon or two to go.

Jim's living room was like an abandoned NASA station. Cardboard boxes, a redundant vacuum cleaner, water bottles and the debris of knowledge everywhere: books, newspapers, magazines, elephants of encyclo-paedias, leaning towers of cassette tapes, newfangled CDs and videos – all the greatest films. There was hardly place for the tiny, veneered press – and not much reason for it either. It was hard to foresee what value this small smidgeon of order would bring to such abominable chaos. But I was happy there. This unlikely pharmacist gave me solace. He made 'mad' interesting. He looked on the abandoned as liberated and could turn every negative into a shining light of hope.

'You should join the drama. Whatever that Tommy Moran taught yez at that school in Drumeela, there's nothing but actors coming out of it. That Brian Reilly and Brona O'Brien – wonderful actors. And, of course, the old guard: Peter McNamee – Peter O'Toole, more like. The presence of that man on stage – he's like a fucking Roman emperor. Jesus Christ, the talent of these people! Quit that auld football and come in some night into the hall. You don't have to take on too much to start with, but everyone can learn. I'm too fuckin' old, really. But you're young. I'm telling ya, it could be the making of ya. You're hardly going to put in presses all your life. And quit that fuckin' drinking. I presume ya drink – watch that drink! It can get in on ya. The bastard of a thing can catch hold of ya and make ya into a useless bollix. It has a hoult of a few in there in Carrigallen; that Aidan Harte and the postman. Don't be one a them.'

Then the shop bell went again and that was that. Jim was gone. I finished up and tidied up, and then I stuck my head into the shop to say goodbye. Jim was with a customer, and the shop was full, but Jim left them all there and walked me out to the van.

'Have a think about that. That drama could suit ya. Otherwise, you'll just disappear … like the rest of us.'

As I drove home, I laughed at what had gone on. I had no intention of trying out for the Carrigallen Community Players, but I was smitten with one of its members – energised by his dramatic take on life. There was colour where I had never seen colour before.

I was back in Carrigallen just after quitting time, parked the van and got into my car. I was almost too excited to go home. I'd go in for one – into the hotel or McGuckian's. For more colour … Sure, why not? I had my day's work done. And the dinner would be there no matter what time I got home.

At lunchtime in Tommy Reilly's workshop a few days later, I was sitting quietly on a workbench. It was Friday and the other lads had all gone down the town for their Friday afternoon treat. I was enjoying the peace. We had had our lunch in the canteen, but the canteen was in a permanent phase of transition and there were no comforts there. Anyway, I preferred the brightness of the workshop, and I've always loved the resting machines of my trade: the table saw, the crosscut, the spindle; the sander and the many drills and routers strewn about the place. And sawdust everywhere – a sense of industry on pause.

I heard the front door open. We couldn't actually hear or see the front door, but the gush of air caused by its opening often resonated through the corridors and made the whole building moan. Who the hell was there? It was too early for the boys – they would be sure to lean hard on the two o'clock restart, especially on a Friday. It wasn't Tommy himself, because he was away. My heart skipped a beat. I hated interruption, especially when I sat idle ... a state much maligned at home. I watched the door into the workshop. No sign of the intruder intruding; it must be a stranger who doesn't know their way around. Then the sound of loose whistling, like my Auld Lad's loose whistling, but in a different key. Then there was 'Hello.'

'Hello,' I said.

'Hello,' again from the other side.

My go again ... 'Hello!'

Eventually, the entrance to the workspace filled with light and a vision stepped in. I say a vision, because in a place and time of great dullness, I was now faced by a man dressed like a chat show host – all cream and bright with a flowery shirt and tie and yellow socks and shiny shoes and the whitest hair. A dangerously clean man with a beaming big smile.

'Hello, there. Could you make me a lid for a teapot by any chance?'

It was Gus Ward from across the way. He lived just over the road in a house – although he didn't look like a lad that came out of a house; more like a character out of a Disney film, standing there in the sawdust of my world. I knew him. Not very well, but he was involved in the underage football in Carrigallen and a big drama man. A great actor and director. But, although he was known for his dress sense, surely this was a little too much for a Friday afternoon!

'Hello, Gus,' I said. 'Are you really looking for a teapot lid?'

'No, not at all. How are ya, Seamus? I was talking to our local chemist, and he said, "Why don't you get that big good-looking fella from Drumeela to join the drama group." So I was just wondering if you knew where I might find such a man ...?'

Digging

I held the crowbar tight. I had a very definite goal. I was going to dig my way out of a hole. We were in the pit of the new milking parlour. The Auld Lad hadn't done a great job with the digger, and I hadn't been very good the night before. I had been drinking and staying out till all hours. Rivers of sweat rolled down my face that morning as I ate my porridge. I wasn't long home. I had gone to a pub question time the night before in McGerty's bar, beside Killegar creamery. McGerty's bar and shop were famous for much, including having no draft Guinness, so I drank pint bottles instead. The bottles had meddled with my innards and left me delicate and faint, and unable to balance myself without dancing on one leg.

I wasn't on a question time team – I would add nothing to a question time team, only weight. I was there as a supporter. Ten pubs from the area battled it out over the course of a few months every year to see who would eventually be crowned pub quiz champions. A community competition which triggered no unity what-soever. Aidan Harte set the questions but didn't always have the answers – which led to more questions and insin-uations and accusations! That night it was McGerty's bar versus the Kilbrackan Arms. A tepid affair till there was a pitch invasion around quarter past twelve. Martin Galagher took out an accordion and spilled several peo-ple's drinks in an attempt to get a tune out of it. Jack McGerty had to bring him home because he was that out of his tree with Smithwick's and bad manners – and attempting to play 'Come Down the Mountain Katie Daly' in the middle of an important quiz. And then the Guards came – they had been tipped off about the small gathering of brains. And while they were in the pub taking names, someone stole the Garda radio out of the squad car. It was an awful act of skullduggery and a new low in the history of the pub quiz. Although everyone knew the perpetrator – a recently acquired delinquent from out of town – there was no point troubling the same Guards with any immediate information. That would only delay their stay. But the whole thing left me so giddy, I needed further excitement, so when the Guards were gone, I set off to a party at the Batter.

There was a go of young ones staying in this old house near Carrigallen called the 'Batter'. They were

over from England planting trees. Crann was an organisation set up by an Australian woman, with a view to
replanting native trees all over Ireland. A wholesome
idea, but more importantly for young lads like me at the
time, it attracted an interesting sort of volunteer to its
headquarters in Killegar. Mostly young women – hippies
and half-hippies with a broad carefree outlook on life.
And they were having a party. I was well cut, but drove
out to this dishevelled house with my drinking partner,
Sean Donnelly. Sean was too old for parties and not
interested in hippies or even half-hippies. But we had a
common longing for beer. There was no beer but there
was loads of gin and vodka and grass. And a bonfire
outside beneath the autumn stars with an abundance
of braless dancing beauties, radiating sultry glances of
intent. I was aflush with wistful vigour and immediately
started moving – swaying – to stay afloat. Swirling in
a sea of lapping flesh and bobbing nipples, I was just
about to sling my hook when I noticed Sean Donnelly
wincing. He had taken exception to my crumbling
moral standing, and he grabbed me by the shirt and
announced that we were leaving – just as the sun was
rising and my heart and hook a-dangling.

I had no problem with Donnelly being so old. Or
wearing his Worzel Gummidge look. Or even having

the limp. But he could be an awful contrary bollix when there was no beer. He said I couldn't be kissing strange women and me with a match at the weekend, and then he had the gall to offer me driving instructions on the way home, telling me to 'Keep out of the egg bushes for Jaysus' sake!' Him that never drove. I always had a fierce soft spot for Sean Donnelly ... but he wasn't doing much for my development as a sex god that night.

I had hardly turned in the bed when Mammy came in all coy, saying that Daddy had made a balls of the digging of the pit for the milking parlour and hadn't dug it deep enough, and never checked it till they had the walls built around it and now he couldn't get the digger in to finish it, so would I help them to dig the last six inches by hand. What a notorious lúdramán this Auld Lad of mine was turning out to be! Why didn't he dig it six inches too deep – it was thirty foot by ten! I hadn't even had an hour in bed and was still full of horrible bottled stout and had just been denied the nearest thing to a ride in over two years. And Donnelly, the dose, would probably be snoring his head off till three o'clock in the day. Him sleeping like a muffin, and me already up and doing the most primitive thing known to man – digging a hole.

The Auld Lad was quiet when I eventually ate my porridge and went out. He said, 'I suppose you had other plans for today?' I said it was okay, I hadn't. Sure, what could I say? He was feeling bad enough. Him and Kevin had to finish doing the things, while I approached the chore alone. First, I sought a positive. The one thing about digging is, it's easy on the brain – my brain was not going to be disturbed for a long while. Hopefully, the digging muscles will work alone. And judging by my mother's softly-softly approach earlier, there might be a sufficient flow of tea and bits to eat. I lifted the crowbar aloft and then engaged with the stubborn ground below.

In Leitrim, the earth is tight. A few inches of soil, if you're lucky, then the daub and then channel – channel like concrete. And that's where I was at! I had a crowbar, a pick, a sledge for breaking stones and a shovel. They were the tools – no brains but loads and loads of thick wit. Thank God, I had that in plentiful supply. I got stuck in. Lift and swing, and poke and prod – hard upon hard doesn't tighten. And then the dancing hippie girls entered into my mind with their uninhibited move-ment through last night's smoky scene – the eroticism of their sinful lure. I had urges to go back and find them there – they would probably be naked now and still dancing – pale against the morning. Why didn't I throw Donnelly the keys and tell him to drive home himself? And I knew he couldn't drive – but for the purpose of my daydream, he drove away, and I was preyed upon by these gorgeous women – English ones with no Catholic guilt – just full of passion and hairy bits.

'How are you getting on?' my father called. I couldn't tell him where I was … in my head!

'Grand,' I said.

'Grand' was our most used word. It meant good, not so good, not good at all and great – it was just a word to replace silence. So, we were mostly 'grand' in our house. The Auld Lad started to dig then – a fierce tidy man with a tool. He made it look simple. All those older crowd could work magic with a shovel or a spade. It was all the practice. Everything was dug by hand back then – spuds, roads, shores – and we dug our neighbours' graves. It was as much a digging convention as it was a practical chore. There was often twenty at the digging of a grave – depended on how well-got the departed was at their time of death. A well-got corpse would have no problem with their excavation. If the corpse was not well-got, there could be as few as two – and two who knew very little about digging graves.

My mind sifted from girls to skeletons. Often when digging a grave, we'd come across remains – bones and maybe the rotting oak or pine of a family member's coffin. There would be a sudden change of atmosphere that came over the diggers. An eeriness of a kind while the bones and bits were gathered and put one side. And the digging of a grave was often a storytelling site. Mostly men taking turns to dig – but also to tell stories. When you got in to dig, you were naturally the centre of attention. And while showing off your skills with a shovel or pick or crowbar, you also had the opportunity to address the gathered audience standing around hanging on your every word. That's if you had the skill to keep them listening. It wasn't unfamiliar to hear howls of laughter coming from the graveyard as the digging progressed. And, of course, there was often a drop of something to lubricate the tongue – and the legacy of a saint-in-waiting to be honoured. But when you got in to dig, your story needed to be good and well told or there'd be another digger thrown in on top of you, and you'd have to get out without finishing your tale with no howls of laughter or cheers – no delight. As small boys and young men, we watched our fathers dig and tell and find the skill of both the digging and the telling, and then it was our turn to follow on – to bury them. And all the while we kept the bystanders at bay with our stories and our need to be the teller if not the digger. In the eighties, we buried many who had us laughing loud ... and some, like my dear friend Kevin

Mitchell, who brought silence to the gathered crowd. But silence tells a story too.

Myself and my father, and later that morning, my brother, joined the digging. We all dug silently – for this was not a grave. More like a burial spot for badly thought-out plans and evaporated dreams. The new milking parlour was a major step forward for Kevin and my dad. My milking days were over – but when the digging was there to do, I dug.

Game over

I couldn't be happier. I was in the County Hotel drinking pints and being hounded by women. Women hoping to get off with a county man. We were after beating Tyrone in a league match in Carrick-on-Shannon. I was back at full back and doing okay. We were blessed with luck that day. A couple of handy goals and we hung on. I was happy out. Yes, because we'd won – but also because I had made a decision. I was going to quit the county. A decision that was coming in a while. I was having niggling problems with my knees and the rest of me wouldn't move ... well, not quick enough for county football. I knew when the championship came around, I'd be lost. I was only twenty-four years old – and unbeknown to anyone, Leitrim were about to embark on the most successful ten years of their history. But I was done. I would play the league and that was it. A weight had lifted when I made the decision. Failing consistently had taken its toll. I was so proud to play for my county ...

but my dream was over. I had done everything I could, but I just wasn't good enough. And in trying, I knew that I had reached higher peaks than if I hadn't tried at all.

I would play the two or three games that were left, but I now knew what I wasn't going to do for the rest of my life. I didn't want to think about the extra time that it would hand me – the empty hours – the lack of direction – and the eventual loss of hope. But all my eggs had been in this one basket for so long and now I was prompting change. Had I any regrets? No. Definitely no. But maybe one. What about the younger me? The boy who practised every day in the field in front of the house – in the shadow of the big ash tree? What would he say? Would he throw away a chance to play Senior for Leitrim – to maybe one day play in Croke Park? I've never regretted calling time, but I often think of him – me as a boy – in my knitted county socks and Blackthorn boots and my head full of football joy. Did I let him down? What did I lose him to? I sometimes see him, at my side, subdued and disappointed with his adult self.

But for now … I was happy in the County Hotel. Alcohol and good-humoured supporters and the kind of girls that only grow on trees and some of them out of their trees. And there was a feisty Tyrone crowd there too. Fresh from recent success in Ulster and determined to make a day out for themselves, regardless of the result. They joined us at the bar, slagging our good fortune, the two fortuitous goals and the fact that their full forward – former All-Star Damien O'Hagan – had managed to get himself sent off. I had been marking him at the time and had convinced myself that it was my stellar performance which had caused his initial frustration, but these Tyrone supporters didn't seem to think so. Said he was inclined to do that anyway – but hinted that I had done okay. I was happy enough with okay.

And the craic pushed us into a corner and brought on the night and then one of them started singing. A well carved-out version of a song – a song that would turn briars to moss – full of pain and suffering, and we bent to its maudlin air. There's nothing like a sad song, well sung, to spoil a bit of craic. So I laid back, filled my lungs and took into 'Take Her Up to Monto' – learned from the endless playing of a Luke Kelly cassette in the car. The loudness of my own voice surprised me – the curious look of the others encouraged me. I was not accustomed to taking centre stage. The song was rousing and humorous and oh so very loud. The bottles on the table were dancing out the beat as babies awoke and the Shannon waters near burst their banks. I had tingles of adrenalin racing through my veins as the whole hotel rose in chorus. And then in final frenzy, they stood and clapped and cheered – louder than for any goal scored earlier in the day.

The next morning, I arrived slightly on time for work. The big door rolled up and the orange van reversed in. A busy staff of three were loading a large cargo for Cornafean. Tommy Reilly was shouting – biting at their heels. They all glanced at me. I was only *slightly* on time. They thought I was going to get a peltin', but Tommy knew better than to bite his only milking cow.

'Ah, Jaysus, boy, look at the head of this fella. You must have been courtin' late.'

Tommy was still under the impression that I didn't drink.

'And Leitrim bet Tyrone yesterday. I heard it on the radio comin' in.' Tommy had no interest in sport; he didn't even know I played for Leitrim. The boys smiled – couldn't believe he was so far off the mark.

'Will ya bring the Wallflower to fit that job in Cornafean?'

The Wallflower of a young lad was tall and long and always lurking. He was from a different universe – a planet called Indifference – and although still a gossan, he had an understanding that there was no hope for effort or sideways thinking. He revelled in the misfortune of those who hoped for better things and especially those who tried.

We drove towards Arvagh. The Wallflower smiled away at his own silent discourse. And after leaving it for as long as he could, he said. 'Were you drinking last night, Seamus?'

I said I was.

'Were you drinking after the match?'

He said this with the disbelief that I might consider myself part of any celebration – he followed it quickly with, 'But sure, you're not really a county man. Don't you only play in the league?

I said, 'I'll soon not be playing county at all.'

That gave him a great lift – confirmed for him that I was a complete flop. He brightened up bigtime.

'Aye, Seamie, you're right! Just concentrate on work – is that it?' He was in his element.

I said, 'You wouldn't know what I'd do.'

He took offence at that. 'No, Seamie, you'll be still working for Tommy Reilly when you're sixty. Still coming in with the big load of sandwiches and going off in the evening to help your father. I've seen it before,' said the lad who had just turned twenty-one.

There wasn't much talk after that … but I was determined that nothing he'd foreseen would ever come to pass.

The following Sunday morning, I said I was going to Mass in Carrigallen. I wasn't. I was going to Carrigallen to be there for after Mass. That's when there was a wee gathering in McGuckian's bar. Second Mass was at half eleven in Carrigallen, and after that it was deemed a natural thing to buy the paper in Pat Masterson's or Paddy McCann's and then stroll up the street and into a pub for pre-dinner drinks. But it wasn't just as dainty as all that. The place would be wedged. Everyone out in their good Sunday clothes and blessed Sunday heads – parched with a thirst for devilment and early Sunday beer. And of course, a 20 box of cigarettes. The smoke throttle pulled down to the last. Ones swinging out of fags. Carroll's, Major and Benson & Hedges – passing them around like they were lifejackets. Noel McLean would pull a guitar from behind his ear and start to sing: 'Peaceful Easy Feeling', 'Me and Bobby McGee' and 'I wish I was in Carrickfergus'. Tears rolling down our cheeks ... from the smoke. Women going upstairs into McGuckian's house to use the women's loo and the men traipsing outside to the men's outside loo. The romantic smell of gentlemen's pee – a steam rising to meet the smog. And then, 'Drink up, Seamie, you won't find three o'clock and Holy Hour!'

There was always music – interspersed with a Seamus Brady poem or a strong fermented fart – both met with rapturous applause and wolf whistles. I was thinking of giving a song a go. I had never sung before in Carrigallen. It was time to give it a lick. I waited for the lull. I thought it would never come. But then – a gap – I once again filled my lungs and made the most of the song I got off the tape. They all looked on in shock. 'When did you start singing?' And, of course, it was porter-fuelled. And of course, musically, it wasn't extremely good – but it was okay. Enough to fill the gap. Enough to say, 'I'm here … I'm still alive. I have something to say and sing about. I refuse to be dismissed by the lookers-on – by the Wallflowers and the clag.'

I told my father that I wasn't going to play football any more with the county. He didn't say much. I told him one evening when we were making feeders in the shed. There was a fancy feeding system bought for the new milking parlour – bought second-hand. It worked, but the feeding drums were rusted through. The Auld Lad knew I'd be able to make new ones to replicate what was there – knew I'd have the time. And he probably thought that it might keep me out of the pub. We were riveting galvanised tin using a hand riveter that was got in Mullen market.

I said, 'You were as well trying to rivet that with your mickey.'

Or words to that effect. Then I told him my news. The complicated nature of our work meant that there was little time for analysing my decision.

He just said, 'Well, sure you know best.'

That was it. I had fought his negativity since I was a boy – only to realise that his negativity was merely his ambition to protect me. Because people like him or me didn't get to ride on dreams. We were meant for repairing and patching up – making the middling good. Working with inferior tools and dodgy knees. And not for the first time, we worked in tandem – knowing each other's every thought … knowing each other's scope … morphing slowly into one.

'This bloody thing better work,' I said.

'Of course, it'll work,' he replied. 'Sure, didn't we only add to what was already there?'

And he was always right. I was simply my father's son.

Van man

I lay splattered on the ground. Underneath my face was
a six-inch concrete block. It hadn't helped the configu-
ration of my head. I had gone to town too early, and
so mistimed my return – got home to Drumshangore
before closing time and the Auld Pair still up. I was
mad with drink and so decided to land the aircraft away
from the house – beside the new milking parlour – and
not join those indoors. I'd wait till they went to bed. I
was twenty-four, so no point in worrying them about
alcohol-related activities. I was an awful mess. Feeling
fierce lonesome in meself – tired from all my growing
up and still finding the world to be a disappointing
scourge. But I became bored sitting there looking out at
the milking parlour. I decided to get out of my aircraft
and stretch my legs – not so shrewd and parts of me still
flying at sixty thousand feet. I had no time to release
the parachute. I plummeted and landed on my face.
Underneath my face? Yes – the concrete block. *Who left*

that there? The block was covered in blood – it must have been in an accident. I hugged myself tight and went to sleep. When I woke up, the kitchen lights were off, and the Auld Pair gone to bed. I erected Seamus into a standing position and steadied the hayshed with his hand. I needed a countdown before I took off for the house. Ten … seven … three and away …! I fell over again. If only I had moved the block. *Who left that there?* I had reached a new low.

In the morning, I woke in my own bed. There was blood everywhere. I checked the mirror and found no one – no one that I recognised. Lumps of skin and half-baked blood falling from my face. I followed the blood out of the bedroom and down the corridor. Everyone was still asleep. I went into the kitchen, and sure enough, it was covered in blood too – and the dinner plate was still out – the only thing that didn't have blood on it – because I had licked it clean. I made a quick scramble to clean up and get away before the cows started roaring for milking time. I cleaned like a man – smearing and dolloping as I went. So I went again and thought *how would Mammy do it?* – but I couldn't remember. Thankfully, I couldn't remember much.

As I silently drove in the direction of 'anywhere but home', I wondered what was up with me. Surely, I wasn't drinking too much? Sure everyone was drinking – I just happened to be good at it. I pulled in at the mart. I sat … I had nowhere to go. This was going to be a long day. I took off again and drove the short distance to the football pitch. I pulled in – parked facing the road – still going nowhere of note. I checked the rear-view mirror to see how my face was coming on. Not good. Also, in the rear-view mirror was the football field. For a split second, it was like seeing an old friend. Then I remembered. Me and football weren't on speaking terms. I had turned my back on it and near forgot.

What would my mother say when she saw the axe-murderous look of the house – the sodden bed sheets and the bloodstained kitchen table and floor? Why was I so determined last night to have my dinner, after bludgeoning myself with a concrete block? What a classic shitshow of a son I had turned out to be. But I wasn't sad. I didn't cry – it wasn't a crisis. Only hindsight paints it that way. At the time, I was simply foraging … seeking out the light in the darkest place. I could have made it easier for myself, but I didn't. I had no map. And with no map – sometimes a lad gets lost.

I made up a story about tripping over my toolbox in the dark. No one believed it except me. So I kept my head down for a few weeks till the wounds started to heal.

They did – they always do. And, of course, my mother was worried about me. And I was worried too – that she might think that it was the hot plate of dinner that made me fall over ... and that she'd stop making dinners! That would be a disaster. So I was good for a good few weeks. Coming home at dinner time and eating with the family. But it was no craic and so I recommenced my routine of calling in for a few pints on the way home from work. The spiral down was on, and it was pulling hard.

One Wednesday evening I got home at seven o'clock and my mother came to the door with my dinner in her hand – said that there was a very important man here earlier to see me. She was preparing to drip-feed me the details for her own amusement.

She said, 'Oh, a very fine well-dressed man ... in a fancy car.'

Both these descriptions could be of anyone out from our own family. Because we thought everyone was better dressed than us and certainly had a better car.

'Mammy, who was here?'

She hesitated as if she had suddenly thought maybe this was not good news after all.

'Are you not going to tell me?'

She left down my dinner and thought some more. 'It was Cathal Farrelly. What would he want with you?

He said something about 'the drama' and a theatre and seats. And he was rambling on. Is he a bit of a bollix?'

I said I didn't think he was, but that I didn't know him well enough to say.

She said, 'He said he might call out to the park some time there was training …' And then she went: 'Did you join the drama?' as if it was yet another pitfall of a caper. But I hadn't.

Jim Williamson had asked me to join the drama. And Gus Ward, the day he came into Tommy Reilly's workshop – but I hadn't the balls to go. Who was I to be getting up on stage with Gus Ward and Aidan Harte and Peter McNamee? They were proper actors – with educations and good jobs. I wasn't going to do that! And it sounded like that's what Cathal Farrelly was after too. So, Mammy's big news was no news at all. I took into the dinner, as she hovered nearby, full of fear. What would the next call from Satan be?

Then – my mother's worst nightmare – the sound of a car outside!

'Oh Jesus, Mary and Joseph, who the frig is this now?' She ran to the window. 'I don't believe it, that bollix is back.' My mother didn't usually curse and her labelling of Cathal Farrelly as a 'bollix' was unfounded. But my mother didn't like mystery. She had initially been excited by this fine, good-looking, well-dressed man – thought that his likes could only bring good tidings. But the more she thought of this 'drama' and them big-shots showing off in the hall – and the drinking and staying out till all hours – the more she was becoming upset at poor Cathal Farrelly standing outside like a lost tourist. 'Will ya go out to that fella. And don't let him in.'

I hoovered up the last of my dinner and went to see what he had to say.

Farrelly was admiring the old house when I got out – and the sheds and the new milking parlour. All positive. He eventually got around to the purpose of his visit. He had an idea. But I didn't have any idea of what he was trying to say. His darting mind, desperately trying to capture the essence of his fantastical vision – a vision with a complicated flight path. Not being a theatre person, I was only picking up some of what he was saying; but it was obvious, he was a man of great passion and foresight and belief ... and the word 'hope' was never mentioned.

They were building a theatre at the back of the community hall. I didn't really know what a theatre was. They needed someone with a van – or access to a van – to bring a load of second-hand cinema seats from the county Louth. Would I ask Tommy Reilly for his van, and would I drive the van some Saturday to transport these seats back to Carrigallen? I said I would. And Farrelly wasn't a bollix – he was a breath of fresh air at the time.

A few weeks later, a gang of able-bodied men headed east, stripped a cinema bare, loaded the orange van and returned to Carrigallen Hall. I reversed up the side of the hall and parked. We were outside what was to become the Corn Mill Theatre. The back door of the new building was opened, and I walked in. I wasn't prepared for what I saw. I was at the back of what is now the auditorium – 30 feet away and 10 feet below my feet was a stage. It had a curved front, matching the curve of the concrete steps that tiered back to me. It was like a Roman coliseum. It took my breath away. Even as a building site, it was drawing me to the stage. I could see performers there – I could even see me there. And I now understood Cathal Farrelly's muddled plan – yes, in one way, it was complicated, but it was also as simple as anything could be.

I went down the steps to the stage. I felt a reverence run through me as I stepped onto the unpainted boards. It filled me with magic – as powerful as it was unexpected. I absorbed the wonder of my surroundings. The others were starting to fire the seats out of the van.

Aidan Harte came in then – a veteran of the Carrig-allen stage. He hadn't been in the new building before either. He too was taken aback by its allure.

He shot his arms to the heavens. 'Hey, hey, ho ho. Is this a dagger which I see before me? The handle toward my hand? Come, let me clutch thee.' And then, 'Is that Mr O'Rourke I see upon a stage? I have never seen that man upon a stage, but for one of green, green grass. Perhaps he will like it there?'

And then Jonathan Finnegan came in and said, 'Come on, boys, these seats won't walk in by themselves.'

My instinct was to dash out and help, but I stole another minute on that stage.

Out on his own

I started working with Christy Kiernan. Christy had a garden gnome quality about him. If you reduced his size and turned him into plaster or concrete and put him along a path, you'd have a perfect gnome. A friendly face, expectant eyes, a button nose, a beard and a hat. But he'd have been wasted as a gnome because he was a great carpenter – and plumber and electrician. An all-rounder who was so busy, he was always somewhere else. But if you got him to turn up, you were elected. He asked me if I would be interested in doing a nixer. I didn't know what a nixer was. I was so sheltered in my little safe nine-to-five working world that I didn't realise there was another world out there with less emphasis on clock-watching and more on making money.

'A nixer – a couple of evenings' work for cash.'

'Oh,' I said, 'that sounds good to me.'

And so, myself and Christy began. We got on great. We'd meet in the hotel after I finished my nine-to-five work, have a few pints, and then go and do another few hours for cash, and then back to the hotel. We were the boys – all measuring tapes and pencils and sawdust in our hair. Like a dating couple with a fetish for wood. I began to appreciate the freedom of being self-employed. I knew the fitted kitchens and wardrobes business like the back of my hand. It would be an easy business to get off the ground. All I needed was a saw – a bench saw. Noel McLean had mentioned to me that he had a marvellous bench saw for sale – a Scheppach table saw – £250 – I could manage that. I could turn the downstairs part of the old house into a workshop. I began to get excited. Was a life-changing plan on the cards? I was keen to get the Auld Lad's opinion, but I didn't have the nerve to spring it on him just like that. I'd bide my time.

I thought that me and him might be off doing some job on the farm some evening, and that I'd bring up the subject of going out on my own then. I could use whatever job we were at as a distraction if his views didn't match mine. Save getting into an argument. Arguing with my father was like slapping yourself with your own fists. He knew me too well, and I would just turn into an incoherent grunting blob if I took him on in an argument. But there was no job to do out in the fields or in the shed. The only time I found an opportunity was one night when he was in the sitting room reading the paper. The *Leitrim Observer*. This was his guilty pleasure – a time when he was relaxed and comfortable. Was it really a good time to bring up life-changing agendas?

My father *owned* the papers – the *Leitrim Observer* and *The Anglo-Celt*. He went to Hyland's shop every Wednesday or Thursday and searched a pile of newspapers left on the counter beside the bread. The names of the regular paper buyers were written on the top-right-hand corner: Sean McKeon, Pat Conefrey, Christy Reilly … and somewhere in there would be Jim O'Rourke. Two papers full of sport and local news. The papers were his downtime – and now he was sitting real comfortable in his chair, reading away at his papers like a studious college graduate the night before an exam.

I went in and sat down. Mammy was in the kitchen. It was just me and him. I stared at the television, which was switched off. He looked over the top of the newspaper – at me and then at the television.

'Are you going to turn that thing on?' he asked.

'No,' I said.

'Good,' he said.

I knew I'd have to just jump straight in – waiting would only cause me to suffocate in his presence. Still watching the blank screen of the telly, I said, 'I was thinking of going out on my own.'

I waited. He pulled down the paper, and instead of looking at me, he looked at the telly too – as if we were both staring at a teleprompter. And the conversation continued. Like two bad actors, we read our lines. He went first.

'Aye, I thought you'd have gone out on your own before this.'

'Could I use the old house as a workshop?'

'Why wouldn't ya?'

'And could I use the trailer as a … trailer … for getting stuff and delivering?'

'You might need to clean it out.' This was going great.

He said, 'Will you not need a saw?'

I said I would, that I could get one for £250.

He said, 'I'll give you the money for that.'

I said 'Oh … thanks.'

And that was it.

This was never going to work – how could it work? He had never approved of anything I ever did before. Why was he starting now? This was going to be a pure disaster. *He thinks I can go out on my own, that I can make it work!* Sure how could it work with a workshop that was once an old kitchen and parlour and delivering stuff in a clatty two-cow trailer – cow dung falling off the lovely presses as I was bringing them into people's houses? What sort of an Auld Lad would allow his son to get caught up in a rat-arsed frigacy like that? And then buying the saw – to compound even further pressure upon me! The voice of reason, me hole. He really hadn't a fucking clue.

The doorbell went off on our front door the following Sunday morning. We were all just home from Mass. A Mass for Granny, and for once in a long time, our whole family had been at Mass together and I hadn't gone to McGuckian's after for the session. Mammy was firing cups of tea in all directions when the doorbell went. It was a very normal doorbell, but like a siren to some. Mammy froze.

'Who the hell is this?'

Anyone who didn't know enough to go round to the back door of our house could only be a nuisance. And she had already defrocked out of her Mass clothes and was all a go-go with tea and whelps of bread and ham.

'Someone see who that is,' was the command. No hint of welcoming the stranger. Daddy didn't answer doors. So it was now down to one of the lesser ones. I went.

It was Gus Ward – coming to see me and he wouldn't come in. He was putting a play together for this new Corn Mill Theatre in Carrigallen and he had heard that

I had driven the van to collect the seats. And although I had passed over the invitation to join the drama before, maybe I would consider a small part in a crowd scene. And that I might help with the set ... and that he was badly stuck. And that was it – that was his pitch. I said yes. I had no questions. I hadn't a clue what he was talking about really, so how could I have any questions? I knew if I went in, I'd find out quick enough what was going on. Gus Ward had a lovely genuine straightforward nature – I knew I was in good hands. He thanked me and I thanked him and then he was gone. I went back into the throng of after-Mass tea and sandwiches in the O'Rourke household. Everyone terribly anxious to know who was that and what did they want? I said who it was and what he had asked ... and they all asked what I'd said and when I said that I'd said yes, a silence fell among us all and I felt their great fear for my soul. Nothing good could come from this. Nothing good could come from that auld drama.

My father sucked air between his teeth like an air filter. My sisters and Mammy went to the kitchen and started doing the dishes. Kevin suddenly had things to do outside. So it was back to me and him again in the same room ... in the same two chairs ... but the teleprompter was out of order for this one. His demeanour different to a couple of days before, when he had blessed my ship of self-employment. What was on his mind?

'I thought you were starting your own business?'

I said I was.

'And how would anyone starting a new business have time for anything other than their new business …? Unless you're only going to make a half-hearted attempt at it. Sure you've never done any acting. What's taking ya into that? How would you have time for that and you with a new business to run? That drama's all right for ones who have nothing else to do. Did ya tell Tommy Reilly you were quitting your job?'

'I did.'

'And what kind of an eejit quits his job and starts a new business, and then joins an organisation that he knows nothing about? And are you not going to play football with Carrigallen?'

'Of course I am.'

'Well, sure you quit the county, I thought you might want to quit playing for Carrigallen too. And where are you going to find the time to make furniture and measure up presses and go for stuff? You'll not find Padraig Corby joining the drama and neglecting his business. I thought you were serious about going out on your own … but sure it's obviously only a cod.'

I walked out – ya couldn't listen to that – I was going to town. My mother knew where I was headed and offered me more tea … brack … sweet cake – anything to keep me from that bloody town. But no one was going to stop me. I had enough. He had drove a stake through my heart – told me in no uncertain terms that I was a complete and utter loser. Even got the dig in about the county – never a man to miss an opportunity to twist the knife. I was red-raw with anger and embarrassment. And, of course, he was right. What was taking me into the drama group? I had nothing to offer. But at the same time, when did joining a community organisation run by a few decent human beings like Gus Ward and Cathal Farrelly become such a fucking crime? I was raging. And drinking 27 pints in Carrigallen wasn't going to make anything any better … but I had nowhere else to go. I was on my own.

God's gentry

The old house was quiet – we didn't go in there much. It hadn't changed since the day we left. We hadn't brought any furniture from the old house into the new one. The new one was all fitted out: fitted kitchen – fitted wardrobes – fitted expectations. There was nothing of us in the new house, apart from the bling. The mantlepieces lined with trophies. Mostly mine for football – shitty bits of marble and shiny tin. Presented at tournaments and pitch openings for second place or just for turning up. And two big ones which took pride of place – one for Leitrim Young Player of the Year 1980 and one for Leitrim Minor Player of the Year 1983. Mammy put them there. I hated them. They were just a reminder of the foolishness of my youth ... chasing dreams like chasing falling leaves. I used to love the October winds as a boy. I'd go racing, trying to catch falling leaves from the big ash tree at the front of the house. It would drive my father mad. 'Such bloody nonsense,' he'd say ... and he was probably right.

I was planning my new workshop in the old house. Simple enough. Take down the partition wall between the parlour and the spare lilac bedroom where Granddad died, and where I got slapped for laughing. Remove the door and returning wall that made up the front porch – basically knock down anything that wasn't holding something up. It still wasn't very big, and the old kitchen cabinet was still there and the press in the corner and the Sacred Heart picture above where Daddy used to sit and the Sacred Heart light. It wasn't suitable at all. There were only a few round-pin sockets. The only thing we needed to plug in when we were there was the radio and the fancy electric knife that Mammy got with the tokens from McCann's new MACE supermarket in Carrigallen. But I had no choice. I had quit my job in Tommy Reilly's, and now, here I was.

The up and down sash windows at the front were covered in spider webs. The dead fly corpses a reminder that entrapment was rife in Drumshangore. The Rayburn range brought back memories of boiling kettles and big feeds, but as fearful as I was of looking forward, there was no point looking back. I started work. I hadn't planned to – but I just got stuck in. I found a sledge and a crowbar in the shed, and I started swinging. I was a natural. I might have been good at making things, but I was twice as good at knocking them to kingdom come. And there was anger in me that helped. Anger at the past and the uncertainty of what was to come. I was swinging in a vacuum – not knowing what I was breaking or what I was trying to build. I got a fire going out the back and I started feeding it with the rubble from the past. Timber, tongued and grooved board, wallpaper, woodworm, doorframes, more woodworm, spiders, spiders' webs, and dead flies. Smoke billowed up into the grey sky for hours, and then I was heading to town with a mighty thirst and a script for a rhyming play called *God's Gentry* by Donagh MacDonagh.

For one who liked solitude, I kept ending up in groups. Football teams, Macra na Feirme and now the new Corn Mill theatre group – once the Carrigallen Community Players. The new theatre was almost ready, but for now, we had to rehearse in the old national school in Carrigallen. It was a very different caper to football. No togging out … no smelly gear … and no running. I hated running. Drama was growing on me already.

God's Gentry was a folk drama with a huge cast. Gus Ward had scoured the countryside looking for young people to join his troupe and so rejuvenate what was once a thriving scene in the area. A hundred years of doing plays, we were told.

'This town has a great tradition of drama, going back to the last century,' Gus explained in a strong Clare accent. He was in Carrigallen for over twenty years, but still held tight to his Clare roots. An inspirational leader of a very new and smoky cast. There were 30 in the room – half of them women, most of them smoking. The Mimnas and the Bradleys ... and Brona O'Brien. Lashings of good-looking girls in the prime of their youth, eatin' fags and blowing scraggly hair from their excited eyes. Way better than football.

The play was set in Mayo about a band of Travellers, speaking in verse and ripping into a song every now and then. I played a lesser Traveller with one bit of a song to sing ... but I was happy out for now. After our first rehearsal, we all went to the Kilbrackan Arms. Way, way better than football. I was a self-employed young bachelor surrounded by these gorgeous women – what was there not to like?

You need certain qualities for self-employment: one – you must be focused at all times. Two – you mustn't take your eye off the ball – in other words, stay focused. And three – work long hours. And if you adhere to these the advantages are: one – you're your own boss. Two – you choose when to work. And three – you choose when not to work. I got it half right – I took advantage of all the advantages and seldom worried about anything else.

I set up my new saw in the kitchen of the old house. It looked odd. It felt odd. The Auld Lad came in to see what I was at. I'm sure it looked pathetic to him, but he didn't say what I was reading on his face.

'That's a good-looking saw,' he said.

I said it was.

'I wouldn't say it's done a whole pile of work.'

I agreed. I said, 'I know it's tight enough in here, but I can just about cut a sheet the long way, so that's the main thing.'

He said, 'There's always a way around these things as long as you're willin'.'

He loved that little caveat at the tail end of a sentence. 'As long as you're willin'.'

I was willing. I wasn't afraid of work. I could horse 8 x 4 sheets of chipboard and ply about like they were Christmas cards – get through mountains of work – when I was working. But I didn't really see the point. I wasn't driven by making money or making kitchens or bog-standard wardrobes. There was no real craft in what I was doing, and without the discipline of a half eight start and a six o'clock finish, I was not focused or anything near focused. I was drifting.

But I loved the play and being in the play and the people involved in the play and the drinks after the play. I felt at home at rehearsal – felt like I knew what I was doing. But it was still only rehearsal. I had yet to walk out onto a stage in front of people. That would be the test. For the month before opening night we went to the new theatre to finalise our moves and run the play. The theatre had its seats now – the seats I had fetched in Tommy Reilly's van. It was simply magic. I couldn't wait for the first night and although I would be terribly nervous, I so badly needed to know if I was up to it. The night arrived. The first play to go on stage at the new home of drama in Carrigallen. The Corn Mill Theatre. And my first time treading the boards in a proper play. I did my bit, said my few lines and didn't mess up.

Then in the second act, it was time for me to sing my bit of a song. I filled my lungs. I was going to let rip. I stepped onto centre stage. Everyone's eyes were on me. What if the song didn't come out? There was a second of doubt. But it did come out. Not only did it come out, but with it a surprising burst of energy and emotion – an expression of youth and longing and calling out to the world: 'What have you got to offer, world? Apart from the misery and despair and the endless ways of tripping me up. What have you fucking got?' I grew ten foot tall as I pranced round that stage ... finding more of 'me' there than I had ever found before.

The show was a minor success. A credit to Gus for bringing us all together – the new theatre a credit too. There was only one thing to do ... celebrate and drink and take every opportunity in the coming weeks to celebrate and drink and even smoke – sure, why not? It was 1989 and we were all part of the new Corn Mill Theatre. Drink and smoke and act the goat like there was no tomorrow.

One sunny Saturday morning in summer, my mother went missing. She had gone off in the car and no one knew where she was. She hadn't gone to work, or the bog, and she never went shopping, and if she didn't come back soon, there'd be no one to make the dinner. It wasn't like her; she wasn't a secretive woman. She returned home at one – she was in her Mass clothes, with a handbag and a prayerbook and beads – and a slightly distant look about her ... not like a woman that was about to make a dinner. She kept looking over at me. I was afraid there was something up ... and there was. She eventually got me on my own.

'Are you in the IRA?' she asked.

'No ...' I said, with a bemused look on my face.

'Well, it must be the only thing you're not into. I was with the nuns in Drumshanbo this morning and they're going to pray for you and I'm going to pray for you because I don't know what else there is. I'm afraid you could be too far gone, but I hope some of us gets strength from somewhere soon.'

I couldn't help but think of poor Mammy driving around Drumshanbo looking for the Poor Clare nuns ... and parking the car and getting out with her bag and her beads and her prayerbook and her good shoes with the bit of a heel ... and locking the car and walking up the little path to the front door of the convent and ringing the doorbell and waiting. The sun shining down and the birds singing and her that wouldn't go to the shop! Her that hadn't that much belief in prayer in the first place. That she'd do that to try and save me – me, who wasn't sure what she was saving me from or if I even wanted to be saved ...

Fickle friends

It's wonderful to get to a point in your life when you think you know everything. And to get there by the age of twenty-four. Especially me – coming from a place where no one knew anything. I strolled into McGuckian's bar at 4.30 p.m., measuring tape in my holster and not the sharpest pencil behind my ear. I removed a full box of Carroll's cigarettes from my pocket; then a lighter; then a modest wad of cash to place on the counter – a left-over habit from the States. A nod to Tommy McGuckian – he knew the Big Man's brew. This evening, I would be sitting on my own smoking fags and drinking pints and being my own self-employed, independent self.

There's a lot to be said for being top of the ladder in a make-believe world. And I felt pity for those who didn't quite make it. Mostly, I felt sorry for ordinary decent people like my father – driving his little Ferguson 135 tractor around the roads – slow as anything – and the big wave if he met someone. Respected by neighbours and being a 'nice man' for all to see. And I felt sorry for my brother, working 18 hours a day and being all decent too. Helpful and digging graves for neighbours and looking for Michael Quinn when he was lost that time, and attending parish socials for all sorts of parish things. And then what about the other decent, boring people? The ones spending days cutting the quick or patching the lane or looking in at a tray of buns in McCann's wondering which one for their tea? Thank God, I was way above all that ... way above.

May and Michael Quinn were brother and sister. She's the one who sat on the back of the Ferguson 20 tractor and went to Mass and nowhere else. But May had to go to the hospital one time with her leg, and Michael was left in the delicate position of staying at home on his own. He had a job carrying out the many instructions left for him by May – notes left all around the house. He had lots to do while she was away. And then, as darkness was falling one evening, he went to look at the cattle and he stepped on a stray sod and that was it. The fairies got him! He couldn't get out of the field that he was in. So, he turned his coat inside out – an antidote to stepping on a stray sod. Maybe he didn't do it soon enough. Maybe he didn't have the right belief – because he became stranded and couldn't find his way home. He sat down on the ditch and lit a fag and died. When they found him three days later, the fag was in his mouth with the full ash still hanging from the butt – never tipped. It frightened some, but they say Michael himself looked calm and peaceful … and dead. Whatever it was that the fairies did, Michael Quinn had a peaceful death.

I was weaning myself off Mass and being good. Helped by hangovers and sleeping in and, the odd time, not coming home. But God was everywhere, and any-where he wasn't, there was fairies or the devil. And the devil was in the drama. That was for sure. In fact, there was a character in that first play we did called Balor of the Evil Eye. He was the devil – and the devil was in every other play too according to some. What else could turn my head so far in the wrong direction? I was spending so little time at work and so much time at these plays and drinking and smoking and singing. And now, making up poems – that was the latest thing. What kind of a young fella, with such a religious dead granny and an uncle a priest and a mother and father who would do anything for anybody, including their children – why would he start writing poetry? Worse still, instead of writing it down and putting it away in a drawer, he was getting up in pubs and saying it out loud.

I was asked to play the main part in the next Corn Mill production, *The Honey Spike* by Bryan MacMahon. I was elated – had the lines learned before rehearsal even started. Turns out, I wasn't that good. Too excited to act. But the leading lady was fantastic. Brona O'Brien – she was playing my pregnant wife in the play. Brona was full of feeling and beautiful stillness. I was like a turkey on stubbles. But at least I knew I wasn't good, and I wanted to learn. Learn about acting – about being in the moment. And I wanted to write too and direct – wanted to be up to me goolies in theatre and theatre people and anything that might take me away from the reality of getting up in the morning and going out to the old house and cutting chipboard and spraying paint and longing for something else.

The Corn Mill Theatre was one of the first purpose-built theatres in the region, and it attracted professional theatre companies from all over the country. I was in awe of these actors and their ability to move me and make me laugh and make me think about important things. And they were the greatest scourge that ever came about any place – turning young people's heads and filling them with all sorts of ideas. But most young people had wit. Most young people didn't bat an eyelid and continued with their studies or their sensible jobs and got on with becoming fine upstanding citizens. Most young people had the brains to know the difference between work and a pastime. Not me. I thought my pastime was my work and that my work was just a necessary evil that I could dip in and out of. I was now a complete and utter fool of a young fella. I once had the world at my feet – a young lad who didn't drink or smoke and went to Mass and helped old people and held onto the tail of his daddy's coat.

The Auld Lad came into the workshop in the old house one day. I was after finishing a television corner unit. They were popular pieces of furniture at the time. He was terribly impressed. It was made from oak-veneered MDF, well finished with a medium oak stain and a cellulose-based lacquer. A press to hold the television in someone's very tidy and sensible sitting room – fitted into an alcove beside an open fireplace. A fireplace with a brass stand for holding the miniature brush and shovel and poker and tongs. I had made a press to put in the most boring house for the most boring hoors sitting like cardboard cutouts on matching comfy chairs and watching *The Late Late Show* and tut-tutting at any mention of sex or craic or ones going out with bishops. I couldn't have any less interest in making that television corner unit, and I was raging that the Auld Lad couldn't see the pointlessness of the whole television corner unit industry. It was up there with bungalow bliss and double-gusset knickers.

'Did it take long to make that?' my father asked.

'No, not really,' I said.

'You could probably make two just as quick?' he said.

I knew where that conversation was going. I was going to town … I didn't need a lecture on 'time in motion'.

'I have to go and pick up stuff before John Reilly's closes,' I muttered.

'Could you not deliver that on your way?'

'No,' I said.

How dare he?

I was beginning to cause a stir in the pubs of Carrigallen – more a disturbance – bursting into song or delivering a recitation or grabbing the attention by whatever means possible. Always the loudest empty vessel, and there was some competition for the loudest empty vessel in Carrigallen at the time. I had also let rip in Gowna and Killashandra and Ballyconnell – getting notions of minor celebrity status. Of course, I hadn't. I wasn't anything. I was just background noise. I think I thought the people listening were my friends, but they were not my friends. How could they be? The pub is no place to make friends or memories. I never made a friendship in a pub that stuck. Nothing valuable in my life ever came out of a pub. And yet all my worst memories were either caused by the pub or drinking too much. We drinking people like the security of numbers – we're fickle friends who give meaning to silliness and stupidity. But it was all I had at the time – like that plant growing out of a seed in a jar. A plant with no soil to nourish it, only the goodness of what it came out of. It can only survive there for a very short while before it needs to be planted. If left without soil and nutrients, it will lean over and die. I was that plant. Among the songs and the fags and the good-ones – the too many pints and the not enough. We didn't look out for each other in the pub, we relied on each other ... because we couldn't look out for ourselves.

My mother worked in the kitchen of the Kilbrackan Arms Hotel when there was a function on. One night my father went in to collect her. There was a dance going ding-dust in the function room and he met with a few people that he knew and was having a laugh. He said he might have a bottle of beer, but he thought the bar was closed. She didn't like to see him sitting there with nothing. So she mustered up the courage and politely asked whoever was behind the bar if she could just get one bottle of beer and an orange for herself. But the answer was no – the bar was closed! Even though she worked there and was worth her weight in gold; even though the tables were full of pints and glasses – she couldn't get a small bottle of beer and a mineral. The one time they found themselves in a bar together. I was there that night. Walked past – well cut – a pint in each hand and surprised to see my mother and father sitting at a table with no drink. I wondered at their situation. My poor mother was ready to cry, my father upset for her. I was hardly in a position to see the sin in that, but I did.

Leaning on gates

The Auld Lad ducked into the old kitchen where I was setting out a cutting list.

'Are ya busy? Could I borrow you for a minute … if ya don't mind?'

I asked what was up.

'Donald Murray's cattle are in our field under Baxter's. Kevin's gone to Killerrin and I could do with a hand putting them back.'

It was the 10th of March 1990, the day before my twenty-fifth birthday. A Saturday. I wouldn't normally work on a Saturday, but I'd been away two days during the week with the Corn Mill at drama festivals. I put on my wellingtons and we walked over the pass at the back of the old house. It was a middling spring day – no rain – no wind – just clouds and a soggy silence between me and my dad. He was very aware that I was only half committed to my self-employment – too aware of my new-found love of theatre.

'How did the play go during the week?'

It hadn't gone great.

'It's a good play,' he said. And then with an informed tone, 'Well, it was a good play fifteen years ago. Maybe it's not what they want to see now.'

The Carrigallen Community Players had produced *The Honey Spike* in 1975 directed by Father Patsy Young. It was a huge success, bringing audiences from all over. The production had moving clouds, moving carts and moving actors – all very impressive at the time. Maura Farrelly and Aidan Harte were in the lead roles. A spectacular production that was the talk of the country. Our latest production of the same play was supposed to get the new Corn Mill theatre group back to those same levels of excellence. But it hadn't. We fell well short of them. We were disappointed. But our disappointment was well diluted each night with pints and sessions and staying out till the road men were on their second break.

My father had been asked to help out at the box office for that first *Honey Spike* in '75 – his only involvement in drama ever. The play took place in the community hall with 350 in attendance. It was the first play I remember being at. As the audience were leaving that night – the night my father was doing the door – people were coming up to him congratulating him and thanking him for the wonderful night's entertainment. He never forgot it. He talked about it for years. The one night he was there, and he got credit. I was pouring my heart and soul into it and, for now at least, I was coming up short.

We found Donald's cattle in the field under Baxtor's looking for grass. The grass in that field liked to play 'hide and seek'. Donald's cattle were pets – quiet and mannerly and they retreated without even one buck-lep. The Auld Lad was delighted. He was sixty-three and not overly enamoured with running off through the cow tracks, chasing after someone else's cattle. Donald Murray wasn't aware that his cattle were out, but my father had made the decision that we'd put them back in ourselves, rather than go over to tell him. He'd prob-ably have to help Donald put them back in anyway, because Donald had no help. Not even a useless son to stand in a gap.

My father had the billhook with him, and he cut a few bushes, and we fenced the hole from where the beasts had come. Handy enough. We were now in the old gardens at the top of Baxtor's field. A viewing point for looking out all over our land. He didn't like to look – so I did.

'There's some view,' I said.

He agreed. I could see him not wanting to claim ownership of what stretched out before him, because he knew it wasn't his. Only his to pass on, just as his father had passed it on to him. But he had improved on what his father had given him. Shored and reclaimed it – knocking many tiny fields into a just few. Manured it – or got his sons to manure it. And now on this dull March Saturday, it didn't look a whole pile.

'Oh now, it's not great land,' he said without any remorse. 'You'd have to go to Meath for that.'

I asked him where the remains of Baxtor's house was and Micky Mac's. He had told me before, but I liked hearing the history and I knew he liked telling it. And if we turned the other way, we could see as far as Ballyconnell and Fermanagh, where he used to work one time.

'That's a lifetime ago now,' he said. And when we turned back, he said, 'I remember being up here the day Joe Hyland came down the road to tell me that you had been born. I forget what kind of a car he had at the time. I saw him turning in the gate and I knew there must have been word from your mother.'

I said, 'And of course you raced down to see what she had.'

He said, 'I don't think I did. I'd say I took me time … I don't ever remember racing for anything.'

My father never strayed too far from the facts ... even the facts that were hard to swallow.

We walked back towards the Sand Park – the field where we sowed our spuds every year. He stopped and leaned across the five-bar gate at the entrance as if there was something to see. There wasn't – only the imprint of last year's crop – and of the year before. Ten long ridges each – the length of the field itself. He was wondering if he should move to lea ground for this year's crop. I couldn't care less. I grew impatient, not to get back to work, but to just keep moving. The act of leaning on gates and staring into the abyss was making me lose the will to live. And I could have gone back alone – I had done my good deed for the day. But something kept me there – something made me stay.

Some sons regret aspects of their relationship with their fathers. I don't. Some regret that they never hugged their fathers. I don't. Coming at my father with a hug would be like coming at him with a sledge. It would crush him ... and me. I loved my father, and I loved NOT loving him. And we had our moments of pure togetherness, without the gloss of rubs and hugs and 'I love you's. And I also loved that sometimes he was my nemesis, my roadblock, my point of anger. Because when I was angry, it was always at myself, but he offered himself as a sacrificial lamb to be slaughtered by his own son for crimes uncommitted – because if he was going to be hated, he wanted it to be by me. And, in love and hate and all the gooseberries in between, we racked up a ton of strength and compromise.

When he eventually heard one of my first recitations, about a father/son relationship ... subtly entitled 'What Kind of an Eejit are Ya?', he passed it off saying, 'Sure, only for me, he'd have nothing to write about.' Rub it in – why don't ya? And the last thing he said to me – 12 years later, as he was getting ready to die, he said, 'You better go back and finish tiling that floor. No point leaving it half done.' And I didn't hug him then either ... and when I returned a few hours later he was gone.

My father and me were different. He was whole, I was only half done. We had the same wiring – the same composition – and we both made things. But while I made things for show, he made things to last. My singing was loud, his was quiet and tuneful. His relationship with my mother was pure and lasting and full of truth, my relationships with women were built on mud.

In the years before my twenty-fifth birthday, during my scramble for existence, within the confines of the pubs and the clubs, and my tentative steps onto stage and screen and the small matter of making a living in the

downstairs workshop of the old house, I had encoun-
tered romance ... well, opportunities for romance
mostly – love or lust or whichever came first. I was never
committed. Never thinking long-term. Only thinking of
me and now. I was paddling away in a pond of plenty –
but what if romance, built on lust, equalled nothing?
What if there was no one out there for the likes of me?

I eventually got the Auld Lad to pull away from the
gate going into the Sand Park and we sauntered back
over the pass – like two priests out for a stroll around
the seminary. Me thinking, wondering if what I had
been up to lately with one young English one was right
or anywhere near right – because it felt right. Or at least
near enough right to continue. I wondered what would
Father Jim, here beside me, think of that?

Suddenly he stopped. Surely he couldn't read my
mind? And he couldn't. He wasn't. He was looking up
the field at the back of the old house. He went to another
gate – another five-bar gate out of the mart stores. He
leaned against it and stood staring at the cows.

'There's one of them round,' he said.

I hadn't noticed. 'Is there?' I said.

'Chancy or there is ...'

We both leaned over the gate like judges – watching intently. The cows were smelling each other for

randiness. Then they danced – a shuffle and a tingle of the toot-toot and the next thing – one was up on the other and the one under was waiting! Of course, there was nothing to wait for because they were all females but she was 'round' all right – she was looking for the bull. This meant I was going to have to give him a hand to put her in the byre or the yard. But wait, another one looking too – or was she? We'd have to wait till that dance concluded to see who was looking for love and who was looking on.

Me and the Auld Lad stood there – watching nature – surrounded by nature. We might have borrowed these fields – named them – helped them as best we could, but nature overshadowed everything we did. It had all the answers – including one for me. Little did I know, as I stood there with my father that day, that I was going to be a father too … a father before the year was out. What would my Auld Lad have to say about that?

Acknowledgements

Thank you to Julie Smith for never doubting, always listening and mostly making it look easy to put up with me. Thank you to Thiernan for your opinion (because I think you might know better than me) and to Jessica and Séalin for perspective and peace. I also must thank my poor mother, Pauline O'Rourke, who hasn't, as yet, asked me to stop this nonsense.

I didn't come up with the title of this book myself. I just don't know who to thank for it. At least six different people said I should call it *Leaning on Gates* – so, if you're one of them, thank you!

Thank you to all the people who inhabit these pages. So many are gone to their eternal reward – I remember you with great fondness. This is a tribute to all those who cast shadows, long and short, on my innocent world of the time. Carrigallen, Drumeela and Newtowngore – don't lose your unique madness, it could very well come back into fashion in years to come.

Thanks to all those who have uttered a positive word – it is never forgotten and worth its weight in gold.

Thank you to Gill Books – without your help, I probably wouldn't have pushed myself to this.

Glossary

The AI man	The man who came to artificially inseminate the cow. Some people called him 'The Bull Man'
billy-o	like billy-o = like the devil
buck-lep (buck-lepping)	leaping like a buck
cat	terrible
childer	children
clatty	dirty, untidy, unpleasant
cold press	press in scullery for cool or cold items
cuggerin	cuddling
dimlick	a softie and a fool
ding-dust	very fast/frenzied/energetically
do the things	chores/work
dunt	push up against or nudge (of suck calves eager for milk)
eejits	fools
egg bush	type of bush with soft white berries
fingerboard	a road sign at a specific crossroads
fluthered	drunk
frigacy	an object or situation of a contrary nature
gobshite	stupid or foolish person, or generally, something bad

gossan	a young country lad
haggard	small plot of land to grow vegetables or a small yard
hoor	annoying or unpleasant person or thing
Leaving Certificate (Leaving Cert)	final state examination sat by secondary school pupils aged 16–18
lúdramán	someone who is a bit stupid/a fool
a mhac	'son' in Irish/a term of endearment
molafuster	an extreme telling off
omadhaun	fool – anglicised version of the Irish *amadán*
Pioneer meeting	Pioneer Total Abstinence Association of the Sacred Heart (PTAA) founded 1898. Members known as Pioneers
press	cupboard
pub question time	pub quiz
a skulk	a chancer, someone always on the lookout for something for nothing
strig	taking the last milk from a cow
suck calf	an unweaned calf
through-other	careless, untidy – 'a through-other type'
well-got	well-liked, well-thought-of
whin	gorse or furze bush